Born With a Silver Fishhook

RON BROOKS

i

For Susan, Tom, David, Sara

and Donna Jeanne, but most of all for my dad

fish·er·man

/ˈfiSHərmən/

noun

> A jerk on one end of the line waiting for a jerk at the other end…

Contents

PREFACE

I have fished for as long as I can remember, and I've written about fishing for the past 20 years. My first recollections are of sitting on

the banks of the old Tamiami Trail Canal that parallels U.S. 41 from Miami to Naples, Florida. It was a family affair back then – I believe I was around three years old at the time – that's me in the picture. I say it was a family affair because all of us went. My dad, mom, little brother, and I would load up in our '47 Chevy Coupe – purchased from a police car auction – and drive into the Everglades a few miles west of Miami on US-41. We made trips from Key West to Miami during the year, and on every trip, we hit "the Trail" for a fish fry.

We were not unlike many other families at the time, and I remember cars and pick-ups parked along the edge of two-laned U.S. 41 between the big Australian pines that grew along the banks of the canal. Everyone was there to catch fish, and just like our family, they were there to catch fish to eat.

We brought with us a big, cast-iron skillet, a bag of corn meal, a three pound tin of Crisco – I believe it was pure lard at that time – and a small metal grate. As we fished and caught small bream, bass, and catfish, my dad would build a small circle of coral rocks, marking the campfire on which we would cook our fish.

I clung to that canal on the trail over the years and fished in it a lot as I grew and went through high school. Even after serving in Viet Nam and returning to Miami, I still fished the canal. It was the place I remember my dad buying me my first, real, fishing lure - a Creek Chub Darter in a frog pattern – from the little tackle shop at Cooper City on the trail. Interesting that in later years, John Cooper, a relative of the original Cooper City settlers, lived across the street from my dad in Coral Gables.

I began writing about fishing late in life. After listening to some of my friends who encouraged me to offer some of my stories to the public, I have compiled this collection of fishing stories, all of them published in a variety of media at some point in the past. They range from humorous to technical, but all of them are true – at least as true as a fisherman can make them. Before I begin, I must preface the whole affair with one, very special article. Once you read that one, you will see some of the flavor of this book, added by the influence of one person. That person was my dad.

My father was a guiding influence in my life. In a lot of ways, he was no different from lots of other dads. In other ways, he was far more special than other dads. Although this collection is not about him, the contents and stories are heavily influenced by him even though he died a long time before any of these articles were written.

What follows is a part of my lifetime of fishing experiences – some of them are hard to believe, but all of them are true.

Ron Brooks

My Dad

Here to start it off is my first offering, a tribute to my dad and all he meant to me:

The long-sleeved, khaki shirt he wore was soaking wet. On an August day with no wind, no rain, and both the humidity and air temperature hovering around 98, he wore that heavy, long sleeved

shirt. He was forced to wear it. Being in the sun for far too many years without protection had taken its toll. Skin cancer and subsequent treatments threatened to end his fishing forever.

He was my dad.

The doctors had ordered him to stay totally out of the sun, something he simply could not do. So he fished undercover - literally. Long-sleeved, khaki shirts, a hat with a sewn-in, cloth, neck covering, and gloves with the finger ends cut out, kept most of the sun at bay.

I used to watch him as sweat dripped off his nose. Behind those huge polarized sunglasses, his eyes watered constantly. If it wasn't sweat running into them, it was the thick coating of sunscreen that caused the irritation.

But, fish he did; and, I never heard him complain.

Back up in a Southwest Florida mangrove creek, early August temperatures on a windless day can be unbearable. We would sometimes sit for over an hour in one spot waiting for the tide to "get right." Swatting mosquitoes and wiping sweat, we sat and baked in the midday sun. And still, he never complained.

There were days in the winter when it was so cold we had to lay down in the boat to avoid the cold wind. There were rainy days that soaked us to the bone, and more often than not ended up giving us a cold. And then there were those days where the weather was perfect. In every instance, the goal was to somehow fish.

We arose one morning at 5 a.m. to drive to Bahia Honda, some 30 miles up the Florida Keys from Key West. It was December, and a north wind was howling as we left the house. We drove all the way up there with him telling me that the wind might not be blowing when we got there.

Needless to say, it was blowing and blowing hard. We sat in the car in 45-degree weather and watched the white caps out toward No Name Key. Then, we turned around and drove back home. I often wondered if he believed the wind would not be blowing. Perhaps it was wishful thinking. We made trips like that more than a few times.

I never knew anyone who loved to fish as much as he. I still don't. I take that back. Maybe my son reaches that level of passion. I thought I did for a long time, but I can't hold a candle to either of them. Oh, I love to fish, but on days when he would launch the boat in a gale, I now stay home.

As I write this, he would have been 97 years old. He taught me to fish, and he helped me teach my boys to fish. He instilled in me a love for fishing that will never die. I think I did the same for my boys as well. At least their wives feel that way most of the time!

I remember the last time I took him fishing in 1995. A stroke had taken most of his speaking ability, and he could hardly walk, but he was so happy – just to be able to fish. I'd give anything if only I could fish with him one more time.

He was my father; he was my teacher; he was one of two great people in my life. He was my dad.

Cane Pole Jewfish

I fished more out of Flamingo than perhaps any other place over the years, most of it with my father. His boat never left the yard in Key West or Miami to go fishing without him either offering me the opportunity to go or telling me that I was going. (I seemed to have been a good anchor boy in my early years!). This one is special. I did get to fish with him one final time:

I grew up in Key West in my early years. I tell you this because it is pertinent to understanding some of this story. You see, a kid living in Key West in the early '50s had nothing to do in his spare time except fish. What time I wasn't fishing, I was thinking about fishing or wishing I was fishing.

We used to go to the little tackle shop on Roosevelt Boulevard in Key West next to the culvert in Garrison Bite and buy a "shiner rig." This shiner rig consisted of about 10 yards of what looked a lot like sewing thread with a hair hook and a split-shot, wound figure-8 onto a wooden matchstick. For a dime, you could get a shiner rig and one whole shrimp for bait. We would sit on the culvert that ran under Roosevelt Boulevard, catch shiners, and take them across Roosevelt and sell them to the charter boat captains. An occasional mullet was sold to the tackle shop for a nickel.

All this to say that fishing was the major activity back then - no television (only those people with enough money to afford a very high antenna could pick up a very snowy Channel-4 from Miami some 150 miles away), and there were no tourists to speak of at the time. Back then in Key West, you were either Navy or Conch, and you never really saw anyone else.

Our "row house" neighbor back then, Mr. Knowles, was a carpenter by trade during the week. It was his son, Willie that I fished, played and fought with most of the time. On the weekends Mr. Knowles turned into a commercial fisherman. He had a 14-foot wooden skiff that he built (fiberglass had not arrived on the scene except as a covering for older wooden boats), and he would fish the inside shoals for jewfish mainly.

Willie told me that after we left Key West, his dad built an 18-foot fishing boat. Old Mr. Knowles began commercial fishing in about 1916 and eventually moved on to carpentry. But he still fished the weekends for jewfish and turtles and crawfish. Back then we called the Florida lobster a crawfish. Apparently, there was no law on taking crawfish because he gigged everything he caught. Willie remembers being in that 14-foot skiff with a sea turtle on its back, crawfish flopping around on the deck and a big jewfish. Mr. Knowles loved his jewfish.

Today they are called Goliath grouper after a politically correct movement forced a name change. I find it rather comical that the new name they chose references the Philistine giant who was a mortal enemy of the biblical Hebrew people! I still call them jewfish.

Jewfish are members of the grouper family that grow to 700-pounds or more. The shoals that old Mr. Knowles fished are those shallow (8-16 feet), areas full of coral, and rocky holes for fish to call home, the perfect place to look for a jewfish.

Mr. Knowles had a gig of sorts, actually more of a flying harpoon, one on which the head would detach from the handle when it struck home. That head was attached to half-inch manila hemp rope. With a glass bottom bucket, he would locate the fish in a hole below and gig him, preferably in the head. The gig head detached from the pole and Mr. Knowles would hand-line the fish to the boat.

On most Saturday and Sunday afternoons you could find Mr. Knowles in his backyard, small as it was, cleaning one or more fish weighing anywhere from 50 to 300 pounds. I think he got about 30 cents a pound, fileted, at the local fish market. I want you to know that a fish two to four times larger than yourself leaves an impression on a ten-year-old boy. It also left an impression on my dad, an impression that quickly became an obsession.

The leaky skiff we kept at Eddie's Fish Basket on Sugar Loaf Key never left the dock without the requisite "jewfish" bucket. It consisted of a hand-line (pronounced rope), heavy wire leader and 12/0-hook all neatly wound into a small, metal pail. Everywhere we stopped to fish that hand-line went into the water with some live bait. It didn't matter what we were fishing for; the hand-line always went in the water. It was at that time that my dad's obsession began. It would be many years before he caught his first jewfish, and the obsession would never leave him.

In Florida Bay, on the north side of the Florida Keys, jewfish were abundant. Shoals, cuts, and inside reefs held some nice fish. That's why my dad and I fished in Florida Bay almost exclusively from the late 50s until his death in October 1995. Florida Bay is fed on the north side from the Florida mainland by numerous salt-water creeks and rivers. These tidal bodies allow water to flow into and out of estuaries, some as large and famous as Shark River, Whitewater Bay or Lostman's River, but most just small creeks going only a mile or so into the mangroves.

These rivers and creeks are the breeding grounds and nursery for any variety of fish, including jewfish. Curiously, jewfish are among several species of fish that are born female and change sex as they grow. Some remain female and some change to male. One study says the number of fish that change is dependent on the surrounding population and changes will occur as required to ensure the survival of the species.

We caught our share of jewfish over the years in Florida Bay. The first was about 80-pounds and was caught in 1959. The heaviest was one weighing 347-pounds, caught in 1967. The last one was 40-pounds in 1990. The ones in between those years are what my memories are made of. Most of the small to medium size fish we caught were caught in the rivers and creeks. The most memorable ones were not the big ones; the most memorable ones were the ones we caught on cane poles in the creeks - no, not shellcracker cane poles, but Calcutta cane poles about 2 inches in diameter at the butt.

Many of you are by now probably saying, "Fish story!" Well, here's exactly how we caught them, beginning with the pole rigging:

Starting about half way up a 16-foot Calcutta cane, we tied a one-eighth inch nylon rope and then looped it all the way to the tip. We tied that to a '00' stainless swivel and to the swivel we tied about 10 feet of the same nylon rope with the terminal tackle on the end. Our terminal tackle consisted of double stranded 120-pound test wire leader with a 10/0 or 12/0 hook and '00' swivel. We loosely wired a 6-ounce weight to the swivel, in such a way that it came off easily during a fight.

Our bait consisted of a small live fish, usually a salt-water catfish with its spines cut off (for our safety, not the jewfish) or a small mangrove snapper. We fished in the creeks and rivers at slack tide. Places like East Cape or Middle Cape canal, Little Sable River and Turner River come to mind. Slack tide is that 30 to 45 minutes where the tide slows, stops, change directions and begins moving again.

The banks on the outside bends in the creek can be as deep as or deeper than the creek is wide, sometimes 12 to 15 feet, and always undercut. Jewfish love to hangout in these undercuts. They are not fast-moving fish, being members of the grouper family, and they hang tight to cover until the current slows and stops. Slowing current is a dinner bell for them and they readily take most live baits presented to them during that slack period. The high, slack tide seems to be best, the theory being that some fish came into the creek on the incoming tide.

Pulling ourselves along the creek using the overhanging mangrove limbs, one of us gently placed the bait down next to the bank and waited for 15 to 20 seconds. If nothing happened, we lifted the bait and let it down a little farther down the creek. We continued this until we got a bite. Someone asked me once how you could tell if you get a bite. Trust me; you know when a 40 or 50-pound fish grabs a bait and runs back under the bank with it! Trust me, you just know! When you feel the fish, there is but one thing to do, and that is to set the hook as hard as you can with the Calcutta pole! You never know what's going to happen next. That, my friends, was part of the fun and excitement! This bite could be a 5-pound baby (which you will promptly launch about 20 feet into the air with your hook set), or it could be a 200-pound monster. I liken the anticipation to flippin' plastic worms or jigs in heavy freshwater bass cover. The hook set there can give you the same type of excitement; you never know how big the fish is until after the hook set!

A fish up to about 60 pounds can be handled and fought with standard cane pole techniques. Over that weight, the fish will begin dragging the boat, and you end up pointing the pole straight at him. Remember, you're using a rope for fishing line. They eventually tire and are easily gaffed and lifted aboard.

My memory takes me back to a time when fishing with my dad was all I looked forward to. My mom used to say that if we weren't fishing, we were either getting ready to fish or cleaning up from fishing.

You may notice that all of this is in the past tense. Oh sure, you can still catch jewfish the same way, but severe commercial fishing pressure on the offshore wrecks and reefs depleted the breeding stock so badly that Florida, in 1992, closed the season on jewfish indefinitely. Over the next five years, they made a dramatic comeback and although the population continues to grow the season is still closed. It just isn't the same anymore. They are now federally protected as well.

I took my dad fishing in Florida Bay for the last time in May 1995. We couldn't fish for jewfish. Even if the season had been open, Pop was no longer strong enough to handle a Calcutta. In fact, he had a hard time even handling a small rod and reel. We fished a shoal area, and I caught several nice mangrove snappers in some really clear water while he watched. As we looked at the baitfish and snapper moving about in our chum line, a small jewfish – maybe 25 or 30 pounds - showed up. We watched him swim through the chum and, with tears in his eyes, my dad waved goodbye to him as he swam away.

We took my dad's ashes to Florida Bay in 1996, my brother and mother and cousin and I did, and we spread them over the shoals where we caught our biggest fish. And with tears in our eyes, we said goodbye to him.

Trout Splatter Poles

A long-time ago, commercial fishing was permitted inside Everglades National Park. They came up from Marathon on the Florida Keys fishing for seatrout in the summer and Spanish mackerel in the winter. The commercial fishermen back then were a special breed...

Once in a great while, even the simplest fishing methods just somehow seem to make sense. We have all of our graphite and composite rods, superior reels, super strong line, fish finders, temperature gauges... Well, you get the picture.

There was a simpler day when gadgets and electronics did not help. Those were the days when a fisherman's senses and knowledge were the best tools at hand to find fish. The old timers knew where the fish would be, on what tide, and for how long they would feed. The really good ones would move with the fish as they made their twice a day tidal feeding migration.

I remember watching with awe the commercial speckled trout fishermen that used to inhabit Florida Bay during the summer. They came either alone or in pairs in old, commercial boats with a cabin, a couple of large ice chests, and a 16-foot shallow draft skiff or two in tow, ready to spend up to a week on the water. They returned only when they either ran out of ice or a place to put fish. They were a very special breed of fisherman.

When we fished Florida Bay, it was not at all unusual for one of them to putter or row over to us to barter for cigarettes. In return for a pack of cigarettes, we'd obtain as many live pinfish, the bait of choice for trout, as we could handle. If you happened to have a six-pack of beer, it got you a cooler full of trout to boot!

Life was not easy for these gruff, commercial fishermen, but watching them at their art was pure joy. They used a cane pole about as long as their boat with a heavy line, three-fourths the length of the pole. A ½-ounce slip sinker kept down a hook tied to a 2-foot leader and swivel. About 2 feet above that was the all-important "popping" cork, a fixture familiar to most trout fishermen.

The idea was to swing the live pinfish bait out the side of the boat as they drifted across the grass flats in anywhere from 3 to 8 feet of water. The popping cork was used to attract the trout to the bait. Trout will move to any commotion on the water and investigate, in hopes of an easy meal. That easy meal was the pinfish underneath the popping cork.

Occasionally, pinfish got scarce, or the fishermen just plain ran out. When that happened, off came the hook and float, and on went the wooden Dalton Special. Now that was a lure! Tying on usually a yellow and white one with some red trim, they used that pole and lure to catch fish. In place of the popping cork noise, they used the end of their long cane poles, "splattering" them on top of the water several times. They followed the splatter with two or three quick, noisy jerks on the Dalton. They said they were "calling the fish" with all that commotion. The combination never failed to produce, and they became known, at least in my world of fishing, as splatter pole fishermen.

The splatter polers I used to watch have long since gone, being replaced by commercial netters, and in Florida Bay, removed altogether since commercial fishing has been banned in most of the Bay. Gone too are the days of coolers of fish being brought to the dock. The current limit on trout is five per person, per day in Florida.

But the memory lives on of how these gruff, salty fishermen made the rest of us look like the amateurs we are at catching trout. To this day, however, if you are fishing for trout with me, don't be shocked when I put my rod tip in the water about a foot deep and shake it like crazy. I'm only *calling* the fish! And, oh, by the way, I do have some Dalton Specials in my box - yellow and white, with red trim...

Catching Sand Worms

An unusual bait for us to try. All we had to do was catch them…

I am reminded of the little boy sitting on the bank of a lake fishing in the winter. He was catching one fish after another in the very cold weather, and the folks down the way were catching nothing. After some time, the fishless anglers asked the little boy how he was catching all those fish. They were not catching anything. The boy mumbled something unintelligible; they asked again, and he mumbled the same garbled words. They asked a third time, and the boy put his hand to his mouth, spit out a mouthful of worms, and said, "You have to keep your bait warm."
With that in mind…

"You have to be fast to keep them from going down into their tubes," said the man. Names escape me these days, but he was a friend of my dad who had taken me, along with my dad, to a big mud and grass flat to catch sand worms. We were in Key West around 1956, and both my dad and I were eager to find a new kind of bait.

What the man, let's call him Frank failed to tell us was that these worms were fast. They lived in a tube they had covered with small shells and sand. The tube is about a half to three-quarters of an inch thick and sticks up out of the mud about 6-inches. You can tell if one is there because his antennae with be sticking out of the tube. But as soon as you get close to the tube, whoosh he disappears into the mud. And the tubes can go down several feet!

Low tide is the best time to hunt for these worms. We were walking around in ankle deep water somewhere close to Key West searching for the telltale tubes. Frank was catching them pretty regularly. My dad and I, on the other hand, were getting wet and muddy.

I tried several tactics, the most successful being to thrust my hand into the mud next to the tube and pinch the tube closed under the mud. This worked about half the time. The other methods did not work at all. I believe Frank, being the experienced worm catcher was much faster than either of us and it showed in his numbers.

In about an hour we had a bucket of worms which Frank split with us. We were going to fish the next day and give them a try.

When we got home with our half-bucket of worms, I reached down to inspect one. I never took the time to see what they were all about when we were catching them. Much to my surprise and chagrin, I found out that Frank failed to give us one more piece of information. These worms bite and don't let go! That immediately made me think I would be using our usual bait the next day and not these worms!

The next day came, and we headed out to Bahia Honda, and our regular fishing spot   I put the bucket of worms in the trunk of the old Plymouth and off we went. I noticed an odd smell but didn't pay that much attention.

When we got to the marina at Bahia Honda, I found out what that smell was all about. It seems Frank failed to offer us a third piece of information, and that piece of information was that we needed to refrigerate the worms to keep them from spoiling. I left the worms in the bucket on our front porch overnight. What we now had was a half bucket of dead, stinking, mushy worms.

We bought bait at the marina for one of the few times and fished anyway. We caught a bag full of grouper as usual on the regular bait we always used.

For some reason, I don't remember my dad ever going back to hunt for sand worms. I know I certainly didn't! And I surely will not try and keep this bait warm!

Why Do They Call Them Snappers?

When a boy from Tennessee comes to Florida to fish, he sometimes does not know what he's about to get into. My cousin found out a few things about saltwater fishing on one trip...

For a country boy, raised in the rolling hills of middle-Tennessee, the first trip to saltwater must have been exciting. For me it was just another fishing day; I was raised on the water. But for my cousin Jim, it had to be something special.

It was summer, and he had brought his new bride, Patsy down to Florida to meet her new "kinfolk." She was a trooper as we fished together for a week. Staying at Flamingo in the Everglades National Park was not the most comfortable of vacations. The cabins had everything a fisherman needed and very little of what a new country wife needed or even wanted for that matter. But Patsy hung in there.

Every year for as far back as I can remember, we made a one or two week stay at Flamingo while friends and relatives took turns coming down to visit and fish. Some would stay the whole time; others would spend a day or two and leave. This year, Jim brought Patsy for what would be their initiation to saltwater fishing.

Summer is mosquito time in Florida, and Flamingo must hold every record there is for the meanest, most persistent mosquitoes around. During the day, if you walked fast and stayed away from any shade, you could avoid being bitten. At night, you took your life in your hands if you ventured out. Going in and out of the cabin door became an exercise in seeing how fast the task could be accomplished. Speed also meant that only a few mosquitoes would get inside the cabin. The lack of speed meant many mosquitoes and lots of rather loud commentary from those inside the cabin!

We mainly fished for snapper on these trips, mangrove snapper. A big one would be 3 pounds; a bragging fish would go 5. Most ran between 1 and 2 pounds. All of the fish went to good use.

We fished with cut mullet strips drifting the flats in Florida Bay. Off Blue Bank and back west to Marker 8 we drifted in water from 6 to 10 feet deep. Occasionally we would catch some pinfish on small hooks and use them for bait, but fresh mullet was the mainstay.

Jim, Patsy and I were fishing one morning and were catching quite a few fish. Patsy loved to fish, but as with most novice anglers needed a bit of help. I baited her hook, and Jim took fish off, as we took turns sharing the "Patsy duty."

As the morning progressed, the fish seemed to get bigger. As an approaching thunderstorm threatened, the fish also became more aggressive.

The cool wind from the storm meant only one thing to me. We either had to make a run, or anchor up and sit it out. Running the 14 miles back to the ramp was out of the question because that is exactly where the storm was sitting. So anchor the boat we did.

It was my father's boat, one made by Brothers Boat Company. They were one of the myriad boat builders who seemed to spring up, build boats for few years and then disappear. To save some money, my father did not purchase a Bimini top. Instead, he found a deal on a big, patio umbrella, the kind that fits in the hole in the middle of a glass table. He fashioned a couple of holders that kept the thing vertical on the boat.

The umbrella had served pretty well in the past during a light shower. It had a tilting option, and you could stay fairly dry underneath it. It was blue and pink, with lots of flowers, and it had 2-inch ball fringe all the way around the edge. I never put it up when another boat was around!

So, there we sat. The anchor rope was all the way out, the umbrella was up and tilted to shield us from the wind, the black clouds were approaching, and we were awaiting the rain.

Jim decided to do something other than sit, so he picked up a rod and cast out the back of the boat. It didn't take long until he had a very nice snapper hooked up. It began to sprinkle as I netted what would be a 5-pound snapper.

At this point, I need to go back to Tennessee for a minute. Up there where I spent all my summers as a boy, we would fish the creeks and lakes for bream, perch, catfish, bass and the like. We had a term we used for the big bream we caught. Fishing in shorts and no shirts – the standard summer uniform – we would occasionally catch a bream that was bigger than our hand could hold. So with one hand on the hook, we pressed the big bream against our bare chest and pinned him there. While we held the fish against our chest with one hand, we removed the hook with the other. Big bream became known to me back then – and they still are today - as "titty" bream. If you told someone you caught a titty bream they knew you had a big one.

Jim took that big snapper out of the net to remove the hook. The wind was blowing harder now, and raindrops were getting bigger and closer together.

Jim was wearing a pair of white coveralls that he brought from his job as a mechanical engineer, and he stood to grab the fish.

Old habits die hard, the saying goes. Jim couldn't get his hand all the way around that snapper, so he did what he knew to do. He pressed the fish against his chest with one hand – just like we did back in Tennessee. Only I don't know a fish in Tennessee with teeth like a five-pound mangrove snapper.

Mangrove snappers have this nice habit of popping their mouths open and slamming them shut faster than you can blink your eyes. They will sometimes snap like that several times while you hold them.

I think it was right about the time the first lightning strike scared Patsy enough to make her scream that the snapper did his mouth routine on Jim's chest. In a split second I had two people screaming – Patsy because of the lightning, and Jim because his snapper had latched onto him. When I say latched on, I mean he bit, with half-inch long canine-looking teeth, right through Jim's coveralls and into his chest!

I think the snapper knew he had hit home because he would not snap again and would not let go! What he did do was squirm and flop as Jim tried to hold him, and that only made the pain worse.

By now the wind was blowing a good 30 knots, and the anchor was dragging. At least the bow of the boat was still into the wind, I thought. The poor umbrella was straining as Patsy held on almost in tears. I think at this point Jim was beyond "almost in tears."

He yelled over the wind to me and asked what he should do. Why was this fish so stubborn, he wanted to know? My reply didn't help.

"That why they call them snappers," I said, and as I did I watched the umbrella swing violently around in the wind and turn inside out.

Now all three of us were getting soaked with rain; Patsy was half screaming and half crying; and, Jim was sitting there staring eyeball to eyeball at his "titty" snapper.

I looked at Patsy; she looked at Jim; then, we all looked at each other and began to laugh. If someone had caught this fiasco on film I think it could have made the evening news!

As quickly as the storm came in, it moved out, and we began trying to organize the boat. Jim just sat with his friend still attached.

It took a good 10 minutes with needle nose pliers and four hands to release Jim from his fish. It took another few minutes to get the fish to let go of the coverall.

Jim is retired now. He is probably reading this and chuckling to himself. We caught a lot of big snapper in the years that followed, and we still fish together from time to time. But neither of us will forget that day he found out why they call them snapper!

The Wonderful Odor of the Flats

When we traveled to Flamingo in Everglades National Park, we could always tell when we were nearing the end of the 40-mile trip through the park. This was especially true if the tide was out and the mud flats were exposed...

I still smell the flats. I can see the mud at low tide, glistening in the midday sun. Small spikes from rooting, mangrove seeds dot the mud, and a long-legged great white heron stalks its prey at the water's edge. A school of finger mullet makes a wake in the shallow water that is now beginning to ebb. I wait as my mind tries to conjure up a big snook striking and sending these baitfish flipping on the mud.

It is low tide in one of the myriad mangrove creeks accessible along the southwest Florida coast in Everglades National Park. It is a sight and smell I've witnessed so many times that today I need only close my eyes to see and smell it all again.

The water is completely off the flats and the redfish and snook that patrol these flats, feeding at high tide, are in the creek as far out as the creek mouth. The shore birds and wading birds are everywhere, poking and prodding in the mud, and fishing along the edge. A pair of skimmers comes rocking down the creek with their lower bills barely in the water leaving a slight trail. One hits a baitfish and breaks formation, swinging high to swallow its catch.

Over my left shoulder, a flock of flamingos, almost looking like they were freshly painted that hot pink color, glides by overhead. Every few minutes a white crown pigeon that migrated up from Cuba or over from the Bahamas flies by at tree top level. They always seem to be flying the same direction, as if they had a rendezvous of some sort. Game birds and considered very tasty in the Caribbean, they are protected here. In fact, all of the wildlife here is protected.

Somewhere on Cape Sable is the grave of Guy Bradley, an Audubon Society warden, who was murdered by plumage hunters in 1905. His death led directly to federal legislation banning the killing of wading birds. I found his grave on Cape Sable a long time ago.

According to somewhat conflicting stories, Bradley was shot while trying to apprehend plumage hunters on the Oyster Key bird rookery, and his body was discovered somewhere near Flamingo. The large key in Florida Bay just to the west of Flamingo is named Bradley Key in his honor. The marker that originally identified the location of his grave is now in the park visitor's center.

I still smell the flats. Like an old friend that beckons me to go fishing, the odor will forever linger in my mind. We used to be able to pick up the smell on the old Ingraham Highway, now a paved road that leads from Homestead to Flamingo. As we approached Flamingo, it was always a special treat to be the first to find the smell. It was a game we played. As a kid, I had some games to play on the way to Flamingo.

As he drove, I would count with my father the number of swamp rabbits sitting along the edge of the road; one hundred and one, one-hundred and two. They were everywhere on the roadside and seemed to be more numerous the closer we came to Flamingo. We counted deer, box turtles, and snakes. Sometimes in the early morning dark, a lightning show from a lingering thunderstorm completely lit up the grass prairie.

Nine-Mile Pond. The last curve in the road that headed now in a straight line for Flamingo was at Nine Mile. We stopped there once. It had been a terrible day, and we headed home early. Normally we fished until the sun was one thumb notch up from the horizon. That meant we had 30 minutes of daylight left, just enough time to make it back to the ramp safely. We stopped to see the last and southernmost body of freshwater on the Florida peninsula. A sign asked us – warned us – not to feed the alligators. As we stood at the water's edge, two very large gators made their way toward us from the middle of the lake. It was obvious they were used to being fed.

Somehow, when it was just Pop and I, I was always the one that counted the most rabbits. I was always the one that picked up the smell of the flats first. Oh, sure – I know why. But it takes me longer to realize some things than I wish it would.

I still smell the flats. I will always smell them when my mind wanders to a time when fishing was great; a time when a boy could be a boy; a time when even a peculiar odor could evoke life-long memories.

The Right Bait

Having the right bait can make all the difference in catching or not catching fish...

Fishermen all have definite opinions about the bait they use. I mean, which of us would try to use a cricket to catch a sailfish? Or who would troll a mullet to catch a perch? We know what we want to use for bait, and anyone who might suggest another option would at best receive a strange look from us.

On a normal foray into the Intracoastal Waterway (ICW) I buy live shrimp, mud minnows, maybe fiddler crabs, or a combination of all three. Of course these would go along with the artificial baits I like to use.

On one particular trip, my wife and I had live shrimp. We were up in a creek that feeds the ICW and had been catching redfish, t rout and flounder on the shrimp. My wife used the live shrimp. The purist fisherman blood in me forced me to use artificial baits.

We had been fishing the outgoing tide in a small feeder creek that fed the larger creek. This small creek is a good place to be until the outgoing tide gets about half low. Beyond that take a chance on not being able to get out of the creek until the tide is half way back in. The fish we were catching were leaving that creek, and to be safe, we left while we still had water under the boat.

We eased out into the main creek to a wide bend and anchored so that we could fish in that bend. The tide was going to slow and stop, meaning the fish probably would not be active until the tide started coming back in. It was a good place and time to make a sandwich and eat lunch. Please notice that I said, "Make a sandwich."

When I fish alone or with another guy, I sometimes only take a few packages of cheese crackers and some soda. At most I will make a couple of ham sandwiches the night before. But, that's about it. I have no chips, no fruit, and no fluff.

But on this day I have my wife with me, and I believe she brought the entire contents of our refrigerator. She laid out a pretty tablecloth on the front casting deck and began constructing sandwiches. I, on the other hand, continued to fish.

To our amazement and joy, there was a big school of seatrout sitting right in the deepest part of the bend where we were anchored. I was catching one on almost every cast, and in short order, my wife joined me in the catching. Being the wonderfully kind person she is, she began talking about how the trout might like something else other than shrimp. I didn't pay much attention to what she was doing.

Then I looked back to see the jig head she was using. She proudly showed me a jig head with the tail of a shrimp and, of all things, a large, green, Thompson grape on the hook. Yes, a grape. I chuckled and made some fun of her activity to which she said something along the lines of "just watch."

I made another cast, and she made one right behind me. I hooked up to a small trout, and to my utter amazement, she hooked up as well. She caught a trout that bit a bait with a grape on it.

I have not been able to live down that trip. Some of the people I fish with know the story because she will proudly tell it to anyone that will listen. And like me, she has a picture of the grape on her jig head.

I'm fishing next week with a good friend. We may troll a celery stick or two for barracuda.

Can It Be Too Cold to Fish?

Fishing in the winter usually meant strong winds and rough water. Somehow at a young age – much younger than I am now – that made no difference…

The first good wave we hit coming out of the entrance channel to Matheson Hammock threw icy, cold, salt spray into my face. Two things are wrong with salt spray. For one, spray in your face means less than calm water. For another, when the spray dries on your face, it leaves a salt cake that drives many people crazy. I'm one of those people. The fact that the air temperature was hovering around 37 degrees made the first two issues all but disappear. It was downright cold!

It seldom drops below 40 degrees in the winter in Miami, but when it does, it can be the most numbing cold an angler can face. Today was one of those days as we headed for the vicinity of marker 23 across Biscayne Bay some 5 miles away. It was cold, I was wet, and the north wind was breathing down our necks at a steady 20 knots.

It's the winter of 1962, and it's mackerel time in Biscayne Bay. While other parts of the country tend to shut down their fishing for the winter, South Florida lights up with the annual run of migratory fish. Biscayne Bay just happens to be the wintering grounds for tons of one of those species, the Spanish mackerel.

The mackerel fishing technique of the day was trolling spinning tackle with white nylon jigs tipped with hard, salted shrimp. Once a hook up was made, we would try to anchor the boat and "jig up" the school. Most of the time the school was scattered, and we simply continued trolling.

The boat we fished out of was a wooden 14-foot Chris Craft open skiff. It was a kit boat that my uncle had built, and it served us for many years in all kinds of fishing. It had three bench seats and a small bow cover. The 10-horse Johnson was a tiller model, and it could get a skier up if there were only one person in the boat.

Today was a day I wished we had stayed at home. As we made our way east, across the bay, every wave we hit would throw spray out from the bow. The north wind would catch it and blow it right back into the boat soaking both of us. By the time we reached marker 23, we were both wet and more than a little miserable.

Times seemed to be different back then. What I look upon now as stupidity seemed perfectly logical to us then. The fish were there, and we had the means to reach them. The logical thing to do was find them!

Trolling meant sitting in the wind, with cold hands on the rod and reel. It meant that the wind would find its way in, around, and under every piece of clothing we wore. It didn't take long for innovation to get the better of both of us.

We caught a few mackerel, and as we sat with numb hands, we both decided we could take the wind no longer. A quick rearrangement of tackle and ice chest left room down each side of the boat.

Almost without speaking, we both decided it was time to get out of the wind. John lay down on one side of the boat; I followed suit on the other. Neither of us could stand it any longer.

The warmth of the sun began to reach our faces as we lay there out of the wind. The boat was rocking, the wind was blowing, and that wind was pushing the light boat along at a pretty fair clip.

I think it hit both of us at the same time as we each took a rod and while still lying down, cast it to the windward side of the boat. It turned out the drift of the boat was fast enough to allow us to drag two jigs along in the water.

As we lay there working our jigs, we both hooked up with a mackerel. Never even sitting up, we fought our respective fish to the side of the boat. A quick sit up to put the fish in the boat, and we tried it again. Friends and neighbors, it was working!

To this day, I think about that trip. How silly we must have looked to any other, larger boats in the area. How embarrassed would I be today to try that?

Youth, I think, brings with it either the courage or stupidity to do some very strange things. I'm not sure which description fits this day, but one thing was for sure. We caught fish!

I remember my father looking at us when we returned home. Our heavy coats, soaked all the way through, reeked of fish smell. It occurs to me now that the thoughts going through my head right now were going through his back then. But I remember telling him as he shook his head that it's never too cold to fish!

Biscayne Bay's Backdoor Trout

Fishing in Biscayne Bay around Miami was phenomenal at one time. Over the years, pollution and overfishing took its toll on the bay. But conservation of the resource and bag limit restrictions have brought this "back door to Miami" back to life...

The ramp at Matheson Hammock was void of people and vehicles when we launched. We seldom fish on the weekend, and this Tuesday morning was like most weekday mornings at the boat ramp. We launched and headed out into Biscayne Bay and turned north for the short run.

For many years in the past, Biscayne Bay suffered under the threat of pollution and over fishing. It suffered so much that lots of people simply quit fishing the bay. New regulations and some great resource management brought the bay back to a fishing haunt that only the old locals recognize.

As a young person growing up on the bay in the late 1950s and early 1960s, I saw very few redfish. The mainstay of our fishing efforts in the bay was the winter, Spanish mackerel run. We would troll white nylon jigs and wire leaders in the area of marker 23 southwest of Key Biscayne. Sometimes the mackerel would be there, and sometimes we would find them right smack in the middle of the bay. When I was much younger, we would anchor so we could catch sand perch from the bottom. Small as saltwater fish go, these little guys fried up quite well, and as children, we loved to catch them.

That was a long time ago. I thought about several of those cold winter trips as we slowed the boat on a recent trip. We were just off the western shoreline in about 6 feet of water. Directly in front of us was Mercy Hospital. The water was clear and the bottom was covered with turtle grass.

Normally, the wind and waves can cause the turtle grass to part with a number of its long leaves, and they float with the current on top of the water. Fishing artificials in this grass is frustrating at best when the grass is floating. But this particular morning, the water was calm and free of any floating grass.

As the boat began to drift across the grass flat, I tied a small jig head on my 20-pound-test monofilament leader and worked a root beer colored grub tail onto the hook. My partner was throwing a shrimp-colored feather jig, one of the many special jigs made in South Florida by a variety of folks, including my dad and me.

We both cast in the same direction off the side of the boat and began working the jigs back with a vertical hopping motion. His jig was taken first, and mine got eaten a few seconds later. Seatrout! Two small trout came to the boat and were released in short order. Two more casts netted one more small trout and one that shook the hook on the surface.

This flat was virtually void of fish way back when. Anyone you saw fishing here was considered a novice that did not know how to fish. Today, however, savvy South Florida anglers fish this flat on a regular basis.

We drifted the flat several times, each time running back and allowing the boat to drift into a little deeper water. Each time we caught a few small trout. As we passed over a small rocky shoal spot in the grass, I saw some fish scatter. I pitched a marker over to identify that spot, and when we cranked to run back and drift again, I slowed to an idle and slowly approached that marker.

We eased the anchor over the side some distance from that shoal and sat quietly for a few minutes. We were close enough to the shoal to see where it was, but far enough away that we didn't spook the fish.

I swapped my root beer grub for a small, red and white nylon jig. I tipped the jig with a small piece of salted shrimp and cast beyond the shoal. As I worked the jig over the shoal, a fish grabbed the jig so hard and fast that the rod almost slipped from my hand. Snapper! Mangrove snapper to be exact. There was a school of snapper over that shoal, and they were hungry. My partner followed my nylon jig plan, and soon we both were tangling with 2-pound, hard fighting snapper on the eight-pound test line.

It was a great morning of fishing. We burned no more than a gallon of gas, and as the crow flies, we were less than a mile from my house! If you had told me when I was 15 years old that we would be catching fish like this in Biscayne Bay, I would have laughed you out of the room. Anyone who fished the bay back then would have laughed at the same way.

But believe it, folks. Biscayne Bay is back, and it's back in spades. There are even some local guides who specialize in bay fishing. Next time you're in Miami, give one of them a shout! Chances are you'll see Mercy Hospital from the water!

The Boat

My father never named his boats. He never thought of the boat he owned as being his. It was always ours, and we always called it simply, The Boat...

In all the years I spent growing up, including my early married years, I never really had to own a boat, not because everyone in South Florida already had a boat (I certainly didn't!), but because I always had a boat available to me.

I think I learned to back a boat trailer before I learned to drive. My dad would give me the car keys and tell me to back the boat into the side yard so that he could reach it with the hose. We all know that he could have backed it in there himself, but he let me do it. I guess I never really realized what he was doing until many years later when I started doing the same thing to my sons. He was teaching me to back in a boat, something I would have to do for myself one day, unfortunately without him.

He let me take the boat without him when I was about 16. I had to sit on a Miami phone book just to see over the dash to drive the car, but he let me do it. Several friends and I would take the boat out into Biscayne Bay and fish or dive for Florida lobsters.

The boat. Notice how it was never his boat or my boat, it was always just, "the boat." Over the years my dad owned many boats - only the last one had a name, the Thea Rachel Marie, mostly after my mom. If I ever talked about buying a boat, he would discourage me and tell me I could use "the boat" any time I wanted. It was just understood that the boat belonged to the family, not to him.

The first boat he owned was one he bought in Key West. It was an old, leaking, 16-foot, wooden, lapstrake skiff that he bought for $100. We caught a lot of fish out of that boat, mostly by trolling. It leaked so badly that you couldn't anchor and fish for more than 10 or 15 minutes without it filling up with water. We would pull the anchor, run fast (as fast as that 12 horse Wizard from Western Auto would push us), and pull the drain plug in the back to let the water out.

He kept the boat tied to some mangroves about 15 miles north of Key West in a creek on Sugar Loaf Key leading to a little restaurant, tackle and bait shop called Eddie's Fish Basket. I think Eddie let him keep it there at no charge if we bought bait there. The boat leaked so badly that it sank in place with its bow tied to a mangrove branch. When we went fishing, it took at least 45 minutes to bail the water out of the submerged boat. I would fish along the mangroves for small snapper while my dad got the boat floating again. I think back and understand now why we trolled the flats for barracuda and never really bottom fished in this boat.

We, actually he, owned six more boats during his lifetime, including a Mohawk, a Squall King, a Brothers, a Thunderbird, a SeaCraft and a Boston Whaler. They were all great boats, and all progressively bigger and better. I have great memories and great stories from every one of them. But none of them were quite like the first.

He sold that first boat in Key West. I remember seeing it sitting on an old wooden trailer right off Truman Avenue at the end of Pinc Street with a sign on it that said "For Sale $75." It sat there for what seemed to me an eternity until someone finally knocked on our door. It seems they were filming a movie in Key West and wanted to rent our boat! The movie director offered to rent the boat for some scenes in the movie for $75.

My dad wanted to sell it, but the movie studio did not want to buy it, only to rent it. So a deal was struck, and the boat was made forever famous in our hearts! I don't remember what happened to the boat after the film, but I do know I can see at least parts of it again. The film is _The Rose Tattoo_, for which Anna Magnani won an Oscar for best actress in 1955. If you ever saw the movie and saw a small skiff on a trailer in the yard, you have indeed seen "The Boat."

Key West Tourist Fish

Fishing from the old Stock Island railroad trestle was something that only a tourist would do...

The hurricane in 1935 that crossed the Florida Keys did not do a lot of damage to Key West. The center went across the keys north of Key West at Islamorada and took out, along with many lives, the central part of Henry Flagler's railroad. Highway bridges and the rail bed on the islands in the middle keys were destroyed, and the railroad never came back. What did stand up were the concrete viaducts that crossed the water from island to island. It was these viaducts that formed the backbone of the new Overseas Highway.

Oh, there was damage in Key West, but not to the extent seen farther north up the Overseas Highway. It was only after the hurricane that the lower keys would be connected to the mainland by road. Before that, a road went from Key West to No Name Key where a ferry would take cars 41 miles north to lower Matecumbe Key.

In Key West, the road heading north paralleled the train tracks to Big Pine Key, but it parted with them there. The train would ride across Bahia Honda channel on the high, trestle bridge from Big Pine Key, while the road took another route across Big Pine to No Name Key and the ferry to Matecumbe. From Key West, the very first bridge was a short one that crossed Cow Key Channel to Stock Island. Built on creosote soaked pilings, the railroad bridge was only about 30 yards to the north of the single lane highway that eventually became U.S. 1. Back then, this was all mangroves and rather remote from the main part of Key West. Stock Island was only minimally developed.

Every time we had relatives or visitors come to our home in Key West, my dad would take them to see what he called the "tourist fish." He would park on the shoulder of the highway where the Cow Creek Bridge began, and then walk across to the railroad tracks. There was no issue with trains on these tracks for they had not seen a train since 1935. A short walk put him and whoever he was leading, out onto the railroad bridge.

Looking down into the water you could see what looked like a maze of snakes or worms or huge ants moving about on the bottom of the very clear, 20-foot deep channel. But, these were not snakes or worms or ants; they were mangrove snapper. Some of the largest mangrove snappers I ever encountered swam under that railroad bridge. I'm not sure whether it was simply the structure of so many pilings or whether the creosote attracted them. Whatever it was, the snappers were thick under that bridge. Curiously they were under the highway bridge, but not nearly as thick or as large as their railroad brethren.

Pop always let whoever he took to the bridge take a fishing rod with him, and he even helped bait and cast if they needed it. What followed was an amazing sight. As the bait with leader and sinker entered the water, the fish parted and formed an invisible circle about 4 or 5 feet in diameter around the bait. They would swim in circles around the bait, but never cross that invisible boundary. It resembled the eye of a hurricane. You could see the bottom clearly in the circle. Pop laughed at the whole scenario, knowing full well that these snappesr had learned not to take a baited hook.

I had one, pretty crusty, old uncle, that visited us on occasion from Miami. He was a bit gruff back then, but he mellowed nicely with age. He fought coming to Key West because he didn't like having to drive 140 miles and also pay the $3.50 toll going and coming back. In the middle 1950s that was a lot of money. I suppose it kept Key West almost void of the huge tourist trade until the toll booths were removed.

This uncle was so bent on catching these huge snappers that he sat out on that trestle all day in the hot sun on one trip. He came back to the house to eat supper, and then went back out there until after midnight. For some reason, we always believed that snapper bit better at night. Well, these particular snappers never heard our theory. He caught absolutely nothing. It was fun going with Pop and whoever he took out there. We didn't spring the tourist fish label until after they had fished for a while. I thought they were pretty naïve to sit and fish for fish that would not bite!

But, I must admit that my fishing buddy and I made the two-mile bicycle ride from our home to that trestle on more than one occasion. We thought we had the right bait, the right way to fish and the knowledge to fool them. Alas, we had none of the above.

On one occasion, while we were on the trestle, my dad happened to drive by on the highway headed home from work. Looking to his right, he saw the two of us out on the bridge. He didn't stop; rather, he waited until we got home later that day. Then he verbally lit into both of us, not for fishing for the tourist fish mind you, but for being that far away from home.

But the punishment of that verbal outburst was soon over, and he was laughing so hard at both us for even trying to catch one of those tourist fish he had to sit down.

I didn't have the nerve to tell him it wasn't our first time…

What Did We Do Before We Had Ice Chests?

It's a smell that never leaves your memory. Dried fish slime buried in a green canvass bag...

I can still smell the wonderful odor of fish dried into the heavy canvas bag. It's one of those smells that, when you run across it, takes you back a lot of years. It takes me back to the times we fished and had no ice chest to hold our catch. This was before we moved from Key West, and back then, our catches could be substantial.

The trunk of the old '49 Dodge was packed with fishing gear. It included the old, air cooled, six-horse Mercury that didn't run very well. Rods protruded from the rear driver's side window, each having been pre-rigged the night before. I was sent to bed early, but my dad and uncle sat up late making wire leaders for bottom rigs. Braided, green, Dacron line was on each of the four old Penn 65 reels and boat rods, tied with a 6-ounce egg sinker to the wire leaders. This was the standard fishing rig in my memory for many years.

It's 5 a.m., and I am half asleep and half excited as we stop at the icehouse on the way to Bahia Honda. The only place to find block ice in those days was the Royal Palm icehouse in Marathon. The tackle shops had not yet taken on ice sales. On the loading dock, I watched as the night attendant hauled a 75-pound block of ice across the wooden floor with his tongs. My dad held open the canvas bag as the ice slid into the opening.

It was a 4-foot tall, round bag, 2 feet in diameter, with a round, flat metal bottom. Drawstrings at the top helped keep the ice from melting. My father mumbled something about high prices under his breath as he paid the 75 cents for the ice – a penny a pound was outrageous for frozen water!

The bag went into the trunk with the other fishing tackle. One more stop for 10 pounds of fresh mullet to be cut up for bait, and we had made the hour drive to Bahia Honda in the Florida Keys. A one-lane road with very little traffic, U.S. 1 ran all the way from Key West to Miami.

I can't remember whether Monroe County ran the little rental concern at the boat basin or whether it was a private operation, but it was there that we rented a 16-foot wooden skiff all day for $5.

With everything in the boat, we headed out into the Gulf side of the Keys, No Name Key on our left and Horseshoe Key dead ahead. We had to stop about every 10 minutes to let the air-cooled engine cool off. It would run until it got hot and then shut down. For the longest time, I thought that was how outboards were designed!

A very unscientific process of triangulation and arguing over which tall tree and which structure on the shore were the right ones to use as targets, was followed by an anchoring exercise. The boat had an old grappling anchor made from lead pipe and rebar, and it took a little practice to get it to hang.

Once we anchored, we pretty much stayed right there for the entire day. That "day" was from sunup until sundown, and we seldom, if ever moved. Heck, we didn't have to move! The gag, red, and Nassau grouper were thick on the bottom. It probably mattered little if we were off the chosen spot by half a mile or so, the fish were everywhere!

And so, the ice bag came to be filled with fish. Seventy-five pounds of melting ice, which surprisingly lasted all day, enough fish to fill the bag, and all of our bottled Cokes, were mingled together in the dark, slimy interior of the ice bag. I can see my father as clearly as if it were yesterday taking one of those slimy 6-ounce Cokes out of the bag, opening it with the bottle opener, wiping the slime with one hand, and downing the entire drink in two huge gulps, fish slime dripping from his chin.

The trip home was one of peaceful sleep for me. I to this day do not know how they drove after being up since 3 a.m. and fishing until six at night. But the ice bag was in the trunk with all the fish and what was left of the ice block. Believe it or not, there was always a chunk of ice left when we got home.

Three hours of cleaning fish put bedtime at around midnight for my father. Completely brown and sometimes burned from the sun – we never used sunscreen – he arose at 6 a.m. to head in for work. How, oh how did he do it? I suspect he could not wait to brag about his catch!
I sometimes wish we still had to fish that same way. It just seemed to be a more special time, a time that required a lot of stamina and patience. And somehow, the rewards just seemed to be greater for all that effort.

Afraid of a Jewfish

I think they may have been fearful of being eaten!

"You go down after him!"

"No, *you* go down!"

"I'm not getting in that water!"

"Well, neither am I!"

The day began as all fishing days did in Key West with a wake-up call long before daylight. The 1952 Plymouth had five or six boat-rods protruding up out of the back seat window on the driver's side. In the trunk were the six horsepower Mercury, a gas can, a tackle box and the canvas fish bag.

Tachie, H.A. and their brother-in-law, my dad, Bud were up and on the road to Bahia Honda to fish. It's only 30 miles, but they would always go on to Marathon, another 12 miles for ice and bait. It seems the ice at the Royal Palm Ice House at Marathon was 2 cents a pound cheaper than Key West. For a 75 pound block of ice they could save $1.50, which could then be used to buy the 10 pounds of mullet they always took for bait. At a nickel a pound for mullet that left them a dollar saved, but I'm not sure it covered the extra gas they burned.

They came back to the marina and store at Bahia Honda, but it was still way before daylight. They sat in the car and waited for the marina manager to come down. He lived in an apartment over the store.

When he did finally come down, he was not the happiest guy on the planet. He usually was able to sleep a little longer. He knew my dad well, because we fished and rented a boat there quite often. Pop always arrived before dawn.

The rental boats were 16 foot wooden, open skiffs with three evenly spaced bench seats. The seats were strategically placed in the boat more for structure than for comfort. Skiff... That's a term given to an uncomfortable boat that is simply a plain boat.

Out of the six or eight rental skiffs, Pop had a favorite. He always wanted the same skiff. I believe that's why he was there so early. See, he had made a couple of subtle modifications to this one over time. First, he mounted a soda bottle opener along the gunnel to open his Coca Colas. If he drank one, he drank a dozen during the day, and all of them went down in one or two big gulps. Second, he had managed to break or modify one of the floor board slats to accommodate the gas can more securely.

Some of the other skiffs had floor boards to keep your feet dry but more importantly to keep you from standing on the inside of the hull; some had no floor boards, and accordingly, they leaked much worse than the floor board models. They all leaked. My dad had picked the one he thought leaked the least to modify.

With the $5 daily rental paid, they loaded up all their gear and headed out into the Gulf side.

The drill for the day consisted of lining up with some landmarks. It was a triangulation effort of sorts that supposedly put them back in the same exact spot on every trip. And because they always caught fish they were convinced they had found that same exact spot. In reality, they could have stopped almost anywhere in the Bahia Honda Channel off No Name Key and caught just as many fish.

Today would be different. Today would be special. And you know what happens on special days. That's when no one brings a camera. Besides, they always waited until they got home to take pictures.

The canvas ice bag was filling up with grouper and porgies and an occasional lost mackerel. I guess he must have been in the area when they cast a bait out and hit it on the way down. These men were meat fishermen. They bottom fished to bring home food for the table. There was nothing fancy about how they fished. A five-foot boat rod had a Penn 65 reel spooled with green Dacron line. An egg sinker was slid up on the line ahead of the swivel and three-foot wire leader. The 8/0 hook held neatly chunked mullet pieces for bait. It was classic bottom fishing.

Only this time it would be different. Fishing only about 3 miles from the dock, one of them got a bite and hooked a fish that he could not turn. As he held on, the fish was taking line out with the drag. They tightened the drag, which slowed the line loss, but caused the boat to turn. Fearing an overturned boat, they pulled the anchor, and the boat moved off in the direction of the fish. They could take in line and get close, but the fish would kick harder and pull more line.

For over an hour they fought this fish. It pulled them from Bahia Honda Channel next to No Name Key to the Seven Mile Bridge. Then it headed under the bridge and out toward the ocean. All three of them were discussing cutting the fish off. They feared they didn't have enough gas to get back in, and did not know how much fight this fish had left! Shades of Jaws!

Suddenly the fish stopped, almost as if it was catching its breath. For 10 minutes it just sat on the bottom. They tried but could not get it off the bottom. Then it began moving again and pulled them back under the Seven Mile Bridge and out into the Gulf. Only this trip was slower. The fish was tiring.

At some point, they were able to bring this behemoth to the surface next to the boat. It was a huge jewfish! The fish was completely spent lying on its side at the surface next to the boat. Lots of hollering and confusion ensued at that point.

About the same time that one of them stuck the gaff in the lip of the fish, the comparatively small hook came out. So here they were with the fish gaffed but not in the boat. The fish was not thrashing, but he was slowly moving. He was slowly sinking, and that wooden handle gaff was their only attachment to it. As the weight increased on the gaff, whoever was holding the gaff laid it horizontally across the gunnel to provide some leverage and to help keep the head of the fish up. Did you see that the gaff had a wooden handle?

41

The inevitable happened, and while trying to leverage the fish, the gaff handle broke. The fish slowly sank to the bottom as the three of them watched.

You could see its outline on the bottom in about 12 feet of water. It was estimated by this crew of fishermen to be around 400 pounds. It died from pure exhaustion I am sure after an hourlong battle with these three goof balls.

And, believe it or not, none of the three of them would dive down to try and get a rope around the fish. They actually left the fish there on the bottom when they headed in.

The version of this story that I heard for many years after it happened was that they had hung a big jewfish, but he "broke off," which I guess could be technically correct since the gaff did break. Not one of them would admit they were simply too chicken to get in the water!

Remembering Father's Day

Father's Day is always a time for me to remember what being a father is all about. And part of being a father is remembering your own father…

I don't remember many specific Father's Days. As I remember it, they took a back seat to other holidays like Christmas, Thanksgiving and Mother's Day. Maybe it was a macho thing. Who wants a holiday named for them?

But, it didn't matter that it took a back seat. It was still a special day and it still meant finding a gift for my dad. That task was harder than you might think, and it became harder as the years went by.

My dad was a fisherman. I don't mean that he simply liked to fish. I mean – he was a fisherman. He ate, slept, dreamed and talked about fishing. The most logical gift every year would be something in the fishing world.

Only, I had a problem with these gifts. I don't know about your father, but my father never waited for someone to give him something. He was not one to hint around before a holiday in hopes of getting watt he wanted as a gift. When he needed or wanted something, he bought it – right then and there.

There was no shopping. There was a tackle shop; it had what he wanted; so, he bought it. Men seem to be that way it seems to me. Except for maybe the eBay phenomenon, men usually don't shop; they buy. That was my dad.

Every year that goes by since we lost him makes me appreciate him more, and not for the obvious things, but for things I find myself doing that fall right into his footsteps. It amazes me the influence he had simply by his presence and how he lived his life.

Not many fishing trips went by as I was growing up that did not include me in the boat with him. He never really invited me to go with him; it was just understood that I would go. Only after I married and moved away from home did I need to buy fishing tackle and equipment. It was just understood that his gear was community property and I used it whenever I wanted.

We fished all over South Florida as I grew up, from Key West to Naples and Palm Beach. Even after I married, I did not buy a boat of my own for several years. I didn't need to have one – I had his.

This Father's Day, I find myself looking at my own children. Children? They're all married, and my two boys are over 40. They both love to fish, and as I watch them and their families, I find myself watching me. I see myself doing the same things my father did with me. And I see them dealing with their children, the same way I did with them. I didn't think about it – it's like it was ingrained in my thinking.

When they were children, the boat seldom left the house without all three of us in it. I bought rods and reels for them, but it was understood that they were "ours."

As they grew older, my boat was always a family thing – not my possession. My oldest son, Tom, with whom I fish today, used the boat more than I did it seems. David moved to another state, but he has one of "our" boats that I did not want to trade, and he fishes out of it every week.

The older each of them gets, the more of me I can see in them. They have children now, and I watch as Tom takes his son, James fishing – teaching him everything he learned from me and my father. David's children are the same way, and I see it in him as well.

There's a point somewhere in all this rambling, and I guess it's this: Whether you realize it or not, as a father, you have more influence on your children simply by being their father than you can ever imagine. My wife sometimes jokingly said that I was acting more like my father every day. I've already heard Tom's wife tell him he was acting like me.

My father was a loving man: a bit eccentric; a bit impatient, overly cautious and truthful to a fault. He had no more quirks than any other aging man. As I think back on how he raised me and what that did for me in life, I have to be thankful. As I look at my children, Tom, David and my daughter Sara, I am thankful once again, thankful that my father instilled in me something that drove me to raise them the same way he raised me.

Was it the fishing that caused all this? Obviously not, though I could make a pretty good argument for that theory. I think it was that he did what we all need to do as men and fathers. He looked out for his children. He taught us right and wrong, good and bad, and he did it with a firm, loving hand.

I miss him this week – heck, I miss him every day. I'm celebrating without his physical presence, but the evidence of his life today is as real as it was 20 years ago. As you celebrate Father's Day this next week, take a good look at yourself, men. Maybe this isn't a holiday for all of us to receive gifts. Maybe it's a holiday made for us to look within ourselves and see just what kind of father we are.

Fishing at Night

All of us will at some point decide to go night fishing – for whatever reason. I have done it and regretted it many times. And- I'll probably do it again before all is said and done…

Imagine what it would be like fishing out here for snapper at night! I had heard that phrase so many times from my father over the years that I became convinced that night fishing was far superior to daytime fishing. It was with those images of monster mangrove snappers that my wife and I decided to fish that night.

While it is true that larger snappers are caught by night fishing party boats, the reality is that these boats are fishing over a reef, not on shallow water flats. Nevertheless, we decided to make a trek into the dark.

We were eating dinner at a table with perhaps the finest water view in the world, in my humble opinion. The Inn at Flamingo in Everglades National Park had only one dining room, but what a dining room it was. After a long hot Day One the water, a hot shower and clean clothes, the air conditioning felt good as we ate our meal and talked about fishing that night. Isn't it strange how a person in a pleasant environment can overlook pending discomfort?

We finished our meal and headed back to our cabin to change clothes. Launching was easy because the crowds at the ramp had disappeared north on the road back to Homestead. It was still light out. The mosquitoes and sand flies had not yet arrived, so our departure was a good one.

We headed straight for Man-a-War channel, a deep cut that connected the flats behind Carl Ross Key (Sandy Key) with the flats across the Rabbit Key basin. We had caught numbers of smaller mangrove snapper along the sides of this cut on many trips. At one time, we even dove there for Florida lobster when they were in season.

I anchored the boat and set up to be able to fish once it got dark. We had only one flashlight, and the batteries on it were weak at best. But, we weren't going anywhere but there, and it appeared that the night would be clear. Star light and moonlight would help.

We began fishing on the bottom behind the boat with live shrimp and cut bait. Almost immediately, fish began taking our bait. I had heard that snapper bite better at night. I guess I never thought about what the other types of fish would be doing.

Catfish. Saltwater catfish. People in Texas call them hardheads. We could not keep them off our lines! About the only thing I ever found them good for was bait for cobia and jewfish. We were going through bait like there was no tomorrow, but I persisted knowing that a huge mangrove snapper was just watching and waiting to take one of those baits.

It's pretty tough baiting hooks and removing fish at night. It's doubly tough when you have to do it for you and the person fishing with you. I was removing yet another catfish from my wife's line when it happened. My rod was in the rod holder doubled over, and the drag was singing that sweet tune that says a big fish is on! I grabbed the rod and began fighting. *At last*, I thought to myself, *the snappesr have arrived*!

As I reeled and the fish fought, it became apparent that this was not a snapper. Long slow runs and dead-weight bottom hugging proved to be a rather large stingray. These are not fun to de-hook in daylight and certainly proved to be more than a handful at night.

We fished for about four hours, caught more catfish than I care to remember, some stingrays, and zero snappers. Discouraged, cold and wet from the dew, we decided to head back in to the dock around 1 a.m.

Because I feared navigating the 14 miles and some of the small cuts through several flats at night, I decided to go the long route out into the Gulf, around Carl Ross and Sandy Key, and then follow the big markers back to Flamingo.

On the northeast side of marker '5', runs a long flat. On the inside of that flat, the water is deep enough at any tide to run east all the way down the shoreline to Flamingo. The trick is getting around that flat. I wanted to run the shoreline because it was a much smoother ride. The only problem was I misjudged the end of the flat.

In short order, we were all but high and dry in less than a foot of water on an outgoing tide. My poor wife was so scared she was crying. Of course, I knew what I had done and that we would float off the flat in a few hours, so I was frustrated, but not worried.

I smoked back then. At one point on the dead low tide, I flipped a cigarette butt out of the boat and it landed about 10 feet away. The water was so low that the turtle grass was out of the water. I watched the red glow of that butt as it burned down, sitting on top of a clump of grass!

Several hours later, the boat floated off the flat, we cranked up, and in 30 minutes or so we were at the ramp. As I idled over to the dock, I figured my worries were over. It was at that point I realized we were in for more grief.

First one mosquito, then another, and then the whole squadron began attacking us. We had to cover our mouth to breathe. I sucked one mosquito right into my nose. It was torture, pure torture getting the boat back on the trailer, but I eventually prevailed, and we ended up back in our cabin.

It took about an hour for my wife to kill, by hand, every mosquito that had followed us into the cabin. With each swat, she had words for me and the dead mosquito. With each dead mosquito, those words were sharper and a little louder.

My wife still fishes with me from time to time. It's not her favorite thing to do, but she has fun as long as two things happen. First, there must be no bugs of any shape or size. Second, she has to catch fish. And she has progressed beyond being happy catching just any fish. The requirement now is the fish has to be table fare. Hard heads and jacks don't count, and very many of them will mean we head for the ramp!

I haven't fished at night in a few years. I'm certain I will forget the problems and issues and try it again in the near future. I'm also certain my wife will not volunteer to be at my side!

This Old Man

This is one of my favorite pieces. I can remember this as if it happened yesterday, and it was well over 60 years ago...

He stumbled a bit as he walked up the gangplank. His slower gait gave away the age he so proudly tried to conceal. Hands, dark and wrinkled from many years in the sun, reached for the railings as he made his way to the stern of the boat. He was just a quiet little man, a mere shadow of what he probably used to be, and all he wanted was a corner of the boat to call his own.

Most head boats, or party boats as some people call them, work on a first come, first served basis. This one was no different. The early arrivals secure a place at the front of the line and thus are assured of a choice spot on the stern from which to fish. But, on this boat, on this day, everyone waited behind an imaginary line on the dock while this little man boarded with all his fishing gear. Some grumbled; most simply waited impatiently as the captain helped the old man tie his rods to the railing on the back of the boat.

When the remainder of the 40 or so anglers were allowed to board, they scrambled to find a spot as close to the stern as possible. Two of those looking for a spot to fish were boys, one 11 years old, and one 9. The 11-year-old was large for his age and passed for 14, the minimum age allowed to board without an adult companion. He was able to push his way in and find a spot for himself. The younger one, on the other hand, got squeezed out and wandered the sides of the boat trying to find that special place.

The old man watched with interest as everyone jostled for position. He listened as anglers told one another why their particular spot was better than the rest. As the boat left the dock, he mused at the stories being told by the regulars about "the last trip." And he studied with particular interest the plight of the 9-year-old boy. Less than 5 feet tall and barely able to rest his arms on the rail, the young boy looked helpless and out of place between two boisterous men. He looked to his 11-year-old friend with sad eyes that said, "Help me!" But it did little to relieve his anxiety. The 11-year-old was too busy gloating over the choice stern position he had managed to win.

An hour ride to the fishing grounds put the boat over an artificial reef, and with considerable jockeying, the anchor was finally sent to the bottom. When the word was passed to "drop your lines," the young boy was tentative as he attempted to put his bait down. The older men on each side of him made no effort to assist and ended up squeezing the boy's already small fishing space into an area that was even smaller.

As he fished from his stern corner, the old man continued to occasionally glance at the youngster. He knew the boy was having a hard time, and the boy knew that the old man was watching, a fact that made the pressure on the boy even worse. Eventually, that pressure became unbearable, and the young boy who so desperately wanted to fish sat back on the side bench next to the cabin. Huge tears welled up in the boy's eyes as he tried his best to mask his hurt. He had saved an entire summer's worth of lawn cutting money to take this trip, and now it appeared he would not even be able to fish.

The old man slowly tied his rod to the rail, told the angler next to him that he would be right back, and proceeded to the side of the boat where the young boy now sat sobbing softly. He sat next to the boy and asked what he had caught, to which the boy quietly replied, "Nothing."

"Well, come back here with me," the old man said as he put his arm around the boy and headed for his spot the stern.

They never even asked each other's name as they began to fish. The old man quietly baited hooks for the boy, removed his fish, and made sure the man in coveralls next to him did not squeeze the young boy out. He helped the boy fight several large fish, and cheered with him as they brought these monsters in over the rail.

I would tell you that they fished the rest of the day together, but actually, the old man never fished again the entire trip. He spent his time helping that youngster gain self-confidence and respect from the men around him. He never complained, never raised his voice - except to praise a particularly nice fish, and he never stopped smiling. All the way back to the dock, the two of them refought every fish several times over. And when it came time to leave, the old man gave the fish to the young boy to take home, a gesture that would be forever remembered.

Sometimes we never know the results of what we do for other people. Sometimes we see a scene like this played out and wonder what the outcome would be for the two people involved.

I can't tell you what the outcome of this day was for the old man, other than the obvious satisfaction he had in helping a young boy. But, I can tell you what happened to that young boy. You see, that young boy was me.

I never saw that old man again and regretfully never even knew his name. That was almost 50 years ago, and I am sure that he has gone to his final reward. I often wonder about just who he was. What special privilege, other than old age, did he possess that garnered him a stern spot on that boat? I used to wonder why he would give up an entire fishing trip just to help a young boy he did not know.

It's only as I have grown older that I have realized the significance of what that old man did for me that day. At the time, I thought he was just too old to fish. But I know now that he gave up his day for a hurting youngster he didn't even know.

I love fishing; I truly do. But as the years pass, I find myself enjoying the experience of just being there as much as actually catching the fish. Maybe my time is coming to help some young boy or girl find their passion. Maybe I realize what that old man was all about. Time will tell, but for now, I'm keeping my eyes open for the opportunity to be a friend to a hurting kid. I owe it to that old man I never knew.

In the Mud

When wading, pay attention to your surroundings. I wish someone else had warned me before this event...

Ah, spring! It's the time that flowers bloom, animals are amorous and most important to me, the flood tides occur. Spring flood tides are an annual occurrence caused by the relative positioning of the sun and moon in the spring, and the effect that this positioning has on tidal movement. High tides can be as much as 4 to 5 feet above normal. Add a good wind in the right direction, and they can be even higher.

Flood tides mean experiencing some fishing methods that are only available once or twice a year. Areas that previously were inaccessible by fishermen are suddenly, albeit temporarily fishable.

So it was on this particular spring morning as John and I left the ramp. The water was so high I had to back my truck all the way past the axle to launch my flats skiff. We were in the Intracoastal Waterway (ICW) headed for a particular oyster bar creek that had been good to us in the past. We were running wide-open doing about 50 knots in the early gray of first light.

I should have seen how big the wake was that the oncoming 42-foot sportfisher was making, but I didn't. We hit his wake and went airborne, jumping probably 6 feet in the air and taching about 7,000 rpm before I could throttle back! I looked over at John while we were midair, and he was flailing away trying to grab anything he could to stay attached to the boat!

Wham! We hit the water and kept running. Bang! John hit the deck of the boat and glared up at me! "It wasn't my fault!" I screamed as he checked for broken parts. "That captain has to slow for oncoming traffic! He's responsible for his wake!" I said.

John just glared and said, "Oh yeah? And just who is responsible for you?"

Onward to the creek. We were trying to catch the high flood tide back in that creek so we could fish a huge flat that is normally crawling with redfish.

I made the turn into the creek and immediately came to a grinding halt. I mean it was a grinding halt! The floodtide had changed the look of the creek so much that I misjudged the entrance and ground my way onto the oyster bar just inside the mouth. And John? Well, John was looking the other way when we hit the bar, and when we stopped, he had rolled all the way to the front casting deck. Boy, can he glare!

As I trimmed the motor up to move off the oyster bar, John got himself back in order. An oyster bar can play havoc on a prop, and this one did just that. I had all three blades, but they now had some new twists and buckles that put an interesting vibration though the whole boat.

You can't run on an unbalanced prop without doing expensive damage to the lower unit shaft and bearings, so I idled up to shallower water, shut down, and tilted the engine all the way up. John just quietly continued to glare at me.

I grabbed some fronds of the sawgrass and held on against the current to keep the boat still. I reached under the console, retrieved my spare prop, and sheepishly held it out in John's direction. BOY, can he glare!

But John is a good sport, and he eased his way over the side of the boat to wade back to the engine. A prop change is relatively easy, but you have to be in the water to do it. As he stood at the back of the boat and began removing the cotter key and prop nut, I noticed that he was getting shorter. The longer he worked, the shorter he got! I knew it couldn't be the tide getting higher because by now it had started moving out.

By the time he got the prop on, without saying a word I might add, he was almost up to his chest in water that was only 2 feet deep!

Stating the obvious, I said, "You must have found a soft spot in the mud!"

Boy, can he glare!

It took several minutes to help him out of the mire. When he did free himself, he entered the boat, covered with really smelly mud and, to both our surprises, only one shoe. I hesitated to complain about all the mud all over the boat. Neither of us mentioned the missing shoe, which was obviously under 3 feet of mud.

We idled back out of the creek to a hard bar where John got back in the water to clean up. John had still not spoken a word.

We finally made it back to that flat we were pursuing, and to our glee, it was swarming with tailing redfish – not your average garden-variety, but some big boys in the 20-pound range. Both of us took our light spinning outfits and eased into the water. We waded over toward a school of reds that had probably 50 fish in it. They were rooting around, tail 6 inches in the air, in 2 feet of water, looking for crabs.

My first cast spooked a big red. John's first cast hooked up with a screamer! His 8-pound test line ran off the reel like sewing thread. Fifteen minutes and several runs later he released a 25-inch red.

My next cast hooked up, and I spent 15 minutes playing mine. This went on for an hour or so until the reds started to move off the flat. I eased over toward the little cut they were using to get into the creek.

As I stood and cast to the oncoming reds, I realized that I was sinking into the mud. Oh, well, with fish coming, who cares? I continued to fish, and my legs continued to sink into the mud.

By the time I realized I was in trouble, John had made his way back to the boat. The water had all but run off the flat, and I was up to my waist in nasty mud. John just sat in the boat saying nothing. It was impossible for him to get to me, and impossible for me to walk to the boat. So I pitched my rod as far as I could toward the boat. It landed reel down and plunged a good foot into the mud. John cracked a small smile.

I did what I had to do, and that was to lie over and begin belly crawling across the mud. Both shoes came off in the original hole, and I looked like a mud puppy squirming across the mud flat. I had to move fast for fear of sinking again. John just sat and watched.

I reached the boat, tried to clean myself off a little bit, and swung over the side into the floor of the boat. Exhausted and smelly, I was a real mess.

John started the engine, pulled the anchor, and began idling out of the creek. He had not said a single word since I had rolled him across the deck of the boat earlier that morning.

As he picked up speed, and I lay there like a floundering whale, I looked up at him. He glanced one more time at me and then broke out into the biggest smile I ever saw. In another minute we began laughing, and in a few minutes we had to stop the boat we were both laughing so hard!

Few people have fishing friends like John and I do. Few people can stand to be with each other through days like this and remain friends. But there we were, muddy, barefoot, except for John's one shoe, and happy because we got to fish together one more time!

Long-Range Fishing Trips
(as told by John Beall)

John and I fished an amazing trip. As John dictated, I wrote it down word for word – as best I could - with some strong editing...

We left May 26, on the *Qualifier 105* boat out of San Diego. John Klein and John Grabosky, two of the best captains around, were in command of a six-day, long-range, yellowtail trip to Cedros and Isla San Benito, two islands off the coast of Baja, Mexico. Thirty-three people were on board plus the crew and all but three were fishing. John and I were part of the fishing group of 30.

We hit the bait barges in San Diego Bay to load up with anchovies and sardines, and then made an 18-hour run to the first stop. We sat through fishing and rigging classes on the way, along with a "safety while casting on deck" course. We started fishing at first light, fly lining sardines with medium tackle. The medium tackle was a 6-foot rod, a Penn Super 4/0 reel with 30-pound test line, and bronze tuna hooks.

We started picking up yellowtails right away in the 20- to 35-pound class. We fished until noon when the skipper came on the speaker and gave us the option of fishing some more here or making a 2.5-hour run to catch bait. John says the secret to catching tuna and yellowtail is good, fresh, lively bait. The secret to getting the most pick-ups on that live bait is picking out the best of the good bait.

"Ya gotta get one that's smilin'," John was told by his mentor on this trip, a nice gentleman he happened to fish next to on the first stop. It turns out this guy's name is Billy Casper. I talked to him and said, "Haven't I heard of you?" He said, "Maybe, I play some golf once in a while." The Saturday after we got back he won the PGA Seniors tournament in Jacksonville, Florida.

At any rate, we decided to make the bait run and sacrifice the fishing for the rest of the day. We made the run and put about 500 brown mackerel in the bait tanks; it took us until 8 p.m. that evening. We caught the bait with a Sabiki rig, six flies on a leader, two leaders for 12 hooks and a sinker on the bottom. Jig this rig up and down. When you get a bite, leave it in the water until it feels like it's filling up. Crank it up and swing it over to one of the mates. He unhooks the fish with the back side of a knife dropping them into the bait tank, and then you do it again!

We made the run back to the fishing spot and anchored up for the night around midnight. It was black bass and shark fishing time for those who could lift their arms higher than their waist. As for John and me, we went to bed.

We awoke to the sound of fish flopping around on the aluminum deck at first light. Up and at them at 5:30 a.m. and we were jigging up bonito, slicing them up and having sushi for breakfast right at the bait board.

A few anglers were seasick. Some were sicker than others. But John and I loved the sushi! We didn't even have any wasabi, but we did have soy sauce!

We got into the yellowtails again. John tried a Sampson rig on the bottom and got a hard bite. He was amidships and got pinned to the rail and dragged to the stern with no recourse but to follow. He got rocked by that one; it's a trick yellowtail like to do. They put their head down and scream for the closest rock. Unless you have a nice Penn International two speed, the fish usually make it to the rocks. Put one of those Penns in low gear and with 60- to 80-pound line, you can turn them.

On the next drop John got my trolling rod broken. Never buy a bargain trolling rod! We switched back to fly lining and had a better success rate. John had had 12 fish by noon, and hooked up one more around 12:30 p.m. He ended up giving his rod to one of the captains, can't remember which one, who cranked it in and thanked him after he finished laughing. He said it was nice to get to fish for once instead of driving the boat.

We went to catch bait again around 2 p.m., another three-hour run back to the bait flats. We fished for bait until midnight. We had a hard time getting what we needed, but we stuck with it. And, so ended a very long Day Two of fishing.

We ran back to the fishing spot and arrived just around first light. Our old hands were so sore we could hardly make a fist, let alone catch bait out of the tank and or put it on a hook. It is now painfully clear why the veterans were taping up their fingers on the first day and wearing gloves to hook up their baits. We had cuts everywhere. However, we didn't pay all that high dollar money to whine, and we only one and a half fishing days left.

We hit the deck as soon as the boat stopped, flipped out a bait and were receives a bite immediately. Some 200 yards of 30-pound test line later, the drag washers on John's Penn reel were starting to smoke. Seals, seals, and more seals; bloody seals were everywhere. You just have to cut your line and take the loss. You can't do anything with them, nor would you want to. They have big teeth.

Out come the seal bombs, (M-80s) and off go the seals for a while. One of the mates put a seal bomb in a mackerel and tossed it overboard. As Heathcliff swooped down and picked it up, his partner tried to get it away from him - boom! Nothing but settling feathers and two gulls swimming feet up. No more bombs stuck in fish - some anglers took offense. Personally, John thought the little flying rats got what they deserved. He had caught about half dozen in the first couple of days of fishing. They would pick up his loose-lined mackerel as it swam on the surface. It's a shock when you get a pickup like that. Your line is going out, and you set the hook, cranking for your life and all of a sudden your line goes up in the air. You just hooked up with Heathcliff, and he ain't going to be too good about coming down and letting you get the hook out!

John had 14 fish the third day; the best one was a 39.5 pounder. One of the mates asked us if we owned a fish market. We were hooked up a bunch and lost way more than we caught.

On the morning of Day Four, we couldn't straighten out our arms when we woke up. Our hands are swollen, and our back and legs were so sore that walking was almost out of the question.

But we hook up with a fish and the pain begins going away. I watched as John was good for four more fish that morning. We packed up that afternoon for the day and a half run back. The total catch was 633 yellowtail for 30 fishermen, averaging 25 - 30 pounds, with the jackpot fish weighing in at 49.5 pounds. John and I each had 33 fish, around 1,000 pounds total weight.

We had one small pickup truck in which to carry around 1,000 pounds of rock hard frozen yellowtail. We called the food bank and donated most of the fish.

Yellowtail won't make you pray to the tuna god at the back of the boat, but they will pin you to the rail and you cannot - absolutely cannot raise your rod up enough to get one turn of the reel on them. You pull up, try to get a turn, get slammed down and lose some more line; you get rocked, re-tie and do it again.

Long-range trips are out or reach for most fishermen, but if you ever get the chance, take it! It is truly the trip of a lifetime!

Two Friends Catch One Very Big Fish

*The jewfish has been politically corrected to Goliath Grouper –
(don't even go there with me). John and I caught a monster with a
tale worth repeating...*

We met at a time that neither of us wanted to meet. I was NCO in
charge of the "Rec" Room in the Marine barracks, and he was
shooting pool. I remembered him then because he was the one who
kept putting his cigarette on the edge of the pool table, and I was the
one who eventually had to boot him out for his smart attitude. I
remembered him that day as pretty much a wise guy.

Six months and a transfer later, we met again when he was
transferred into my outfit. Over the next few months, we would grow
to be best of friends while we hunted, trapped muskrats and fished
together. He was from Iowa and knew his stuff when it came to
hunting and freshwater fishing. I was from Florida and
complimented the saltwater side of the equation. When my Marine
tour was up, and I returned from Vietnam, I got out. When his tour
was up, he stayed in and made a career of it, retiring in 1987 as a
captain.

Did you ever fish or hunt with someone whose every move you
could predict? And at the same time, he could predict yours? Well
to this day we have that simpatico. When we're in a boat, we each
seem to be able to move and act almost without comment and do the
things that need to be done; we are always in the right place with a
net or a gaff, always setting an anchor with just a nod, and always
able to move over and under each other when we both have a hooked
fish.

I have dozens of stories about our fishing trials and tribulations, and
maybe they will eventually all come out of my archives. But this one
trip was something special.

It was 1972, and John had taken some leave to visit me in Miami. We took off for Flamingo in Everglades National Park, where my dad had set up housekeeping for two weeks in one of the park's fully equipped cabins. Of all the times we had previously fished together, we never had a chance at a jewfish. John had heard all the stories, seen the pictures, and had even helped me make some leaders out of aircraft control cable. But never had we fished for one. But this trip gave us the opportunity.

We had the tides estimated perfectly as we followed the slack tide from east to west. It was on marker 6, a five pole pyramid marker south of Carl Ross Key that we had finally anchored. We hooked a live snapper on the 12/0 hook and handline, and pitched it toward the bottom of the marker. We had just let the rope settle and had a slip knot tied in it, when the rope began to move steadily out and under the marker

Both of us reacted to the rope, and as I moved to start the engine, John grabbed the rope to tie it off on the starboard aft cleat. I started the engine, John tied off the rope, and we tried to slowly move away from the marker. The idea was to keep the fish from wrapping up in the marker. Only, the fish had other ideas!

As I increased the throttle, the boat slowly moved back toward the marker and eventually was right on the marker. The fish had pulled us instead of us pulling him!

We saw immediately that the fish had moved straight through the marker and was heading away from it on the other side. As we tried to figure out what to do next, the fish turned and started back to the marker.

"Here he comes!" shouted John as he began taking in the rope. "He's headed right back for us!" Both of us knew what that meant, and within a couple of minutes, the fish had managed to do what we both had feared. He had wrapped himself around several of the poles at the base of the marker. The rope was now tightly locked to the marker.

We knew the fish was still on, because his huge tail was boiling water on the surface as he tried to free himself. After several minutes, we decided that we needed to somehow unwrap the rope before it could be cut by all the barnacles. John untied the rope from the boat cleat (a BIG mistake!) and climbed up on the cross-arms of the marker. As he moved around the marker with the loose end of the rope in his hands, he was turning white - literally. You see, this marker was a seabird roost, and was covered with their white excrement.

As I watched John's apparently futile attempts, I failed to realize that the boat had drifted away from the marker. It was right about then that I heard John telling me that he had the rope freed and that the fish was headed away from the marker again!

I scrambled to get the engine started and then realized that the anchor was out. So, while we both were screaming and I was pulling the anchor, I watched John standing on the marker helplessly trying to put pressure on the fish before the rope ran out!

But, as has happened so many times between the two of us, we got lucky. About the time I got the anchor up, the fish stopped and turned again. John was saved from a sure swim because I know without a doubt that he would never have let go of that rope.

We got that fish, and even though this picture is old and worn, you can see just what a bruiser he was.

I am sure that John will read this story. We still keep in touch, and our friendship lives on. I wonder if he has the same feelings running through his head reading it as I had while writing it. Friendships come and go, but true friends last forever. John, if you are reading this, Bud, keep the faith!

Spending a Night on a Boat

John and I also did a bit of night fishing. We planned to cook fish on the boat – and naturally, we knew we would catch fish…

At several points in every fisherman's lifetime, some things have to happen. They happen to every one of us, and we all learn valuable lessons. The list includes things like hitting your partner in the head with a sinker, hooking yourself when you cast, dropping a rod overboard - well you get the picture.

Like all men, not being as wise in our younger years, we fail to realize when one of these events is about to occur. So it was with John and me when we decided that we needed to spend all day, all night, and all day the next day fishing out of an 18-foot open boat. We had all the right reasons for this foray, things like, "the fish bite better at night," and "it will be a lot of fun." Isn't it amazing how we seem to overlook the obvious when we are about to do something dumb?

I remember in grade school when we were going to "camp out" in the woods next door, we took everything we needed and put all of it in a pillow case, one that to this day, my mother does not know about. "Everything" meant a pound of bacon, the kitchen skillet, and a whole bunch of candy bars. Why we thought we needed to fry, bacon is still beyond me.

In this case, our "everything" included flour, cornmeal, 2 gallons of oil, salt and pepper, a skillet, a very old Coleman stove, a huge jar of jalapeno peppers, a box of Ritz crackers, and a ton of Pepsi's. Never did things like forks, spoons or plates enter our mind. All we saw were fresh fish filet's being fried and eaten literally within minutes of being caught. Talk about fresh fish! I can remember saying that over and over to myself.

We left very early; I believe 4 a.m. rings a bell. We always had to get there early. I think that's because the mosquitoes are always thick early in the morning, and it just wouldn't be fishing without those mosquitoes to complain about. The destination was Flamingo in the Everglades National Park. Flamingo sits right on the tip of Florida and offers access to Florida Bay and all of the estuaries surrounding the tip of Florida.

The day was not unlike other fishing days - nice weather, light wind. Except that I now firmly believe that the fish knew our plan. We were relying on our catch to feed us for three days. "Talk about fresh fish" - remember that phrase?

I guess it was sometime in the afternoon of that first day that John and I finally talked about the impending problem. All through the day as we fished, we each thought about the problem, but neither of us would talk about it. Oh, we talked about a lot of things, but never about the fact that we were not catching any fish! I can't remember whether it was John or me that decided to broach the subject.

We were back behind Carl Ross Key (it was named Sandy Key at the time) off markers 9 and 10 and stone crab traps dotted the water as far as we could see. Being very subtle about our situation, I said, "You know, there are crabs in those traps, and they probably would go well with the fish we're going to fry."

John's reply was just as subtle, "Yeah, kind of a nice appetizer."

It was after we had pulled about a half-dozen traps that we realized they had just been run and baited and had not been down long enough to catch any crabs. But on the last trap, our luck changed! There, inside the trap, in all its beauty was a small jewfish. It couldn't have been more than 5 pounds, and it had entered the trap to feed on the crab bait.

We looked at each other and smiled, and our stomachs immediately began growling. I eased open the trap, took the fish in one hand, closed the trap, and dropped it back into the water. It was just as I raised the fish for John to admire that it happened. Do you know how slippery a jewfish is? One flip, one bounce off the rail, and one splash later that little jewfish was swimming free!

It was almost dark now, and we headed for Man-O-War channel to anchor. All plans to fish the places we had originally dreamed about were dropped. The task at hand was dinner, and fast!

We anchored in the channel and set a couple of rods out as we contemplated what we were going to eat, each of us wondering separately if one particular species of here-to-fore junk fish would be good to eat.

Suddenly, one rod went down and just as quickly the other bent double. Two nice mangrove snapper came up - and both stayed in the boat!

A minor circus of sorts followed the catch as we began preparing to clean, filet and cook these two self-sacrificial offerings. The stove was setup on the big ice chest. Flour and cornmeal came out, and the fish filets were ready in no time. Soon the sizzle of fried fish was heard, and the smell was wonderful.

"These two filets are done," John said, "hand me the plate."

Remember that pillow case I told you about?

"Well that's OK, we'll just eat them right out of the skillet," I said, "Get us a couple of forks."

Remember the pillow case?

Have you ever tried to eat flaky fried fish in the dark, out of a hot skillet, with a pocket knife? It's not too bad if you aren't really hungry and you keep your tongue off the sharp edge. We managed to eat the fish, and in fact, caught a few more that we cooked. We had our dinner and sat back to relax.

Relax. Two things happen on a still night on the water. First, mosquitoes from neighboring mangrove islands are drawn to any light. Once you learn that and get bug spray in your eyes, the second thing starts happening - dew. Do you have any idea how wet an open boat can get from dew in one night?

Well, we did not fish long the next day. It was back to the ramp, boat on the trailer, and head home. We had made enough stupid mistakes for one trip. So, on the way home, to prove we were smarter than we looked, we decided to have a jalapeno pepper eating contest. Remember the pillow case? The rules were simple: No swallowing them whole - you have to chew them, and the first one to quit loses. I ate one, and then John ate one, and so it went until we ran out of crackers and Pepsi. We never did finish the jar of peppers.

I have not been able to eat jalapenos since that trip. I also avoid all night fishing trips, unless the night is spent in a hotel room! And, by the way John, I still say I ate more than you!

Big Bull Dolphin for John

John and I fished for dolphin – the fish not the mammal – on many occasions. This time we finally got a good one for him to brag about...

The country was at the mercy of Fidel's random act, for he had inexplicably decided to allow boatloads of Cubans to flee their country in any craft available. They were floating in the Gulfstream for miles like a rag tag parade of boats. Relatives from South Florida made the 90 mile trip from Key West to Mariel in larger boats in hopes of finding and claiming brothers, sisters, mothers, and fathers.

John was a captain in the Marines, an avionics officer at the time, and he was in Homestead with a detachment of reconnaissance F4 phantoms for two months. They would evidently fly recon missions over the straights while the boatlift was underway.

It was not a crisis as far as we were concerned, so the world event that brought us together again became a welcome chance to do some fishing. We had not fished together for several years. The Marines had taken him on another WESTPAC tour, and I had settled into my family raising duties in South Florida. The time and distance between us had been all too long.

This particular Saturday found us together on the water once more. Homestead Bayfront Park was the closest launch site for us, and we were there at the break of day. We had the boat with us and the weather forecast was perfect.

We spent the evening before pre-rigging fresh ballyhoo on 6-foot wire leaders and 7/0 hooks. The ballyhoos had been caught by a commercial bait-fishing friend and were in an icy salt brine. The salt brine made them firmer and easier to work with than fresh bait, and not only were they the freshest in South Florida, they were free!

Just off the mouth of Caesar's Creek, marking the shallow reef is Pacific Light. Not a real light-house, but a large metal structure, it lies between Carysfort Lighthouse and Fowey Rocks Lighthouse. So through Caesar's Creek and out past Pacific Light, we went, in search of the blue water and a good weed-line.

I often use terms like "smooth as glass," or "like a lake," to describe a particularly calm day. Today was one of those that needed a good description. There wasn't even a ground swell to break the endless horizon.

We ran probably 10 miles off the reef, past the southbound shipping lanes and toward the middle of the Gulfstream. Southbound ship traffic always runs just inside the stream to avoid its 6-knot northerly

current. Northbound traffic rides the middle to take every advantage of the extra push. We found a small weed line of Sargasso and put out our baits.

We were flat-line skipping two ballyhoos, one on each side of the boat. We trolled for only a short distance when we saw some floating wooden debris away from the weed line. I eased the boat that direction to see if we had some company under the wood.

Before we could get there, we both saw him coming out of the water. A bull dolphin (a male mahi mahi), probably 30 pounds or so, was off the starboard bow about 200 yards away and heading toward the baits. He was airborne twice as he streaked toward the skipping ballyhoo. We call it "crashing the baits" for a reason. He hit that first 'hoo from the air and immediately grabbed the second bait! But somehow, he missed the hook on both baits!

With our hearts racing, we stopped the boat and began reeling in the flat lines. As we did, we noticed that the water around the boat was teeming with small dolphins. We immediately picked up our pre-rigged spinning gear and started catching these "grasshoppers" on chunks of ballyhoo.

As I reeled in a schoolie, I noticed a large form lurking just out of casting range. It was that big bull dolphin, and he was staying out there watching the other fish. I put a whole ballyhoo on a spinning rod that I could cast and tried to bring him in closer. He paid no attention to it on the first few attempts, but then he finally nailed the bait.

We fought and landed that bull, and this catch made up for all the lost time the years had put between us. We would fish together several more times during those two months, but none of the trips would be quite like the first - a perfect day, a perfect ocean, and two good friends reliving their time together. It probably would have been just as special even if we had not caught any fish. The fact that we did, made it even better, and John got his big bull.

John Beall 1948-2004

After all the fishing we did together, getting this news was one of the worst days of my life…

There is a time that comes to all of us at some point in our lives that makes us have to sit back and assess where we are and where we have been. All too often, we press on with our day to day lives not thinking of things that could have been or things that may not come. Then something happens that kicks our eyes open and makes us sit up and take notice of everything around us. That happened to me this past weekend.

My Sunday morning email jolted me into reality. A short note from my best friend John Beall's email account hit me like a brick. It was written by John's roommate, and it simply said that John had died Saturday. There were no details. I think the lack of details made this even harder to accept.

All of you who follow my articles know John. I've written about our fishing escapades over the years. We fished together more times than I can remember over the past 37 years, even though our individual lives took different paths. Our common bond was a love for fishing, the outdoors and each other.

John was probably the best technical fisherman I ever met. He knew every nuance of lure movement and bait presentation. He could manage to catch fish when no one else could. And it did not matter where or on what body of water he was fishing; he always had a handle on the fish.

We trapped muskrats together while we were stationed in North Carolina in the Marines to earn some spending money. John knew all there was to know about the outdoors in my eyes.

We fished the rivers, creeks and coastal waters of North Carolina together. Even though he was from Iowa, he knew how to catch saltwater fish. I have pictures of him and his son, Nick, then a toddler, with stringers of bluefish and seatrout.

We fished the lakes and rivers of the Midwest, from Des Moines and Red Rock to Table Rock. I remember one trip where we caught no fewer than 30 bass on spinnerbaits, all from one single point below the Red Rock Dam in Iowa.

We chased up pheasants from his Aunt's corn field in Iowa one summer. The corn was so high I only heard them; I never saw one fly. Then we snuck over a small rise in the cow pasture as I listened to him tell me stories about how many ducks he had taken over the years from the farm pond just over the hill.

We deer, squirrel and dove hunted. The first dove hunt I was ever on was with John. I went through two boxes of shells without hitting the first bird. The first deer I ever killed was with John. I shot at it 16 times with a .22 automatic before it fell. I hit the deer with eight of those shots. At that time rim-fire cartridges were legal where we hunted.

We mounted a couple of squirrels together one year. We mailed off to Herter's and got the glass eyes and spent one entire Saturday practicing our taxidermy skills. I still have that squirrel 37 years later.

The stories of our times together could go on for a long time, with lots of laughs and more than a share of disbelief from most people.

I fished with John this past March at Toledo Bend in Texas. John was living in San Diego and me in Florida. He drove from there, and I brought my boat from here. We stayed together in a cabin at Lowe's Creek, fishing for almost a week. We talked about old times, about all the things we had done together and then about the things we had done away from each other. John had overcome some issues in his life, and it appeared he was finally going to do well. It was good to be together again.

There are reasons for everything, I suppose. And there are some things that happen that we may never understand. John's death is one of those I think will never understand.

We had planned to fish on Lake Okeechobee for a week this spring. It's a trip we made several times in the past with several other people, and he so looked forward to it. This time it would be just he and I, fishing together again. The shellcrackers would be bedding and as John put it when I last talked to him, "We need to do a little 'perch jerking.'"

I will make that trip this spring. And, I'll jerk a few perch while I'm there. But it won't be the same. One seat in my boat will be empty, although it won't be as empty as that place in my heart. John was a good man and a good friend. He is gone and that hurts me. I shall miss him.

Square Grouper and Bull Dolphin

Trolling off South Florida could bring almost any surprise you can think of...

Spring is dolphin time in South Florida. The run of fish begins around the end of April and lasts until the "dog days" of August. Before I go any further, let me restate the name of that fish. Mahi-mahi, or as they are called on the West Coast, dorado, are the pelagic fish known as dolphins in South Florida. They are not related to the mammal family of dolphins! I have to clear this up because readers from all over the world complain that I might be catching "Flipper"!

We were trolling off Pacific Reef out of Homestead, Florida, halfway between the southbound and northbound shipping lanes. The Gulfstream runs about 5 to 6 knots in a northerly direction, and southbound ships try to stay on the westerly edge, so they are not impeded by the current. Northbound ships take advantage of the current and try to run dead in the middle of the stream.

It was midmorning when I saw the floating plastic. I had not seen any plastic in quite a while. It was a square bundle of black plastic floating half way down in the water. Square grouper! In the '70s and '80s, we used to see them all the time. Some anglers were foolish enough to try and bring one on board and take it back to the dock. This, my friends, was a bale of marijuana! They were so common many years ago that anglers jokingly said they were going fishing for square grouper. I even have a silly looking tee-shirt depicting one of these strange fish.

Today, and even back then, we were smart enough to leave the floating bale alone. A quick call on the VHF to the Coast Guard with some LORAN numbers would bring one of their boats to pick it up, but not before we were through with it!

As I passed a short distance from the bale, I saw what I was looking for - two big dolphins just hanging out underneath. Dolphin will sit under any kind of flotsam to get out of the sun. The blue water is so clear, and the sun penetrates so deep that finding shade is tough. Weed lines, old boards, - heck, I even found one sitting under an old toilet seat one trip - anything that floats and takes away the sun will attract them.

I made the first pass rather wide, and the fish did not react to the bait. On the second pass, I sped the boat to run what we call "hot baits," and managed to bring the two ballyhoo skipping on the flat lines within about 10 feet of the bale of dope.

Both fish erupted from under the bale and came out of the water. If I had been ready with my camera, I would have had a pair of fish completely out of the water, each with a ballyhoo in its mouth. What a beautiful sight!

We caught both fish. The big male was around 40 pounds, and the female weighed in at about 30. We went on to catch quite a few more dolphin, mostly along weeds-lines. One school of grasshoppers (the little guys) stayed with the boat for over an hour while we broke out the light tackle.

Oh yes, I forgot about that bale. As soon as we caught those two big fish, I took a LORAN reading and called the Coast Guard. They took the information, and I left the area! I never did see them come out from Miami to look. I guess one bale in a sea of so many more was not worth their effort!

Everyone Needs a Charlie

Charlie is a fishing machine – the ultimate outdoorsman and someone I look up to with great respect...

A 2-foot chop greeted us as we made the turn out of the entrance channel and headed into Biscayne Bay. I sat on the back side of the cooler rigging a couple of ballyhoos as Charlie put the SeaCraft up on a plane and pointed her at the entrance to Caesar's Creek.

Charlie. Every angler should have a Charlie in their life at some point. Charlie was and still is the quintessential sportsman. From fishing South Florida to hunting caribou in Canada, Charlie was about as good as they come.

He grew up to pilot seagoing tugs in his father's business. I believe the Atlas and Wood tugs out of Miami were two that he captained. Pushing and pulling cargo barges up and down the East Coast of the U.S. and into the Bahamas and Caribbean, Charlie had seen a lot of the sea in his life. Some of his stories of cargos and ships' crew pushed the edge of the believability envelope, but they were fun to hear, and he loved telling them.

We fished together and hunted together in South Florida for many of years. I remember one duck-hunting trip where we both pulled, and simultaneously fired, on the same bird in a flock on three different occasions on the same morning. The "discussions" around the ownership of those three ducks continues to this day.

Caesar's Creek was as it always was this early in the morning – slick as glass and crystal clear. We made the bends in the creek, passing the gathering of anchored sailboats to the side. A favorite nude anchorage at the time, we sometimes surprised a young couple taking an early morning dip.

As we broke out into the channel that winds its way into Hawks Channel on the ocean side of Elliot Key, the sun was breaking just above the horizon. Clouds of orange and red hue parted the sunrays as we crossed the reef and Charlie backed the engine down to accommodate the 3-foot seas.

We looked for a weed-line as we headed for the edge of the Gulfstream. Sargasso weed lines are common in the 'stream, and to a dolphin (mahi mahi) that means a food laden expressway on the water. We hit the deep blue water indicating we had found the edge, but we didn't find a weed line. A current rip was evident though, and Charlie idled down and angled the boat alongside.

We only put two rods out when we were dolphin fishing. There was no need for anymore. If a school crashed the baits, two rods were all we could handle anyway. In the fall we might add one more rod with a trolling feather and a handlined downrigger plane. Wahoo and blackfin tuna seemed to like that feather better than a skipped ballyhoo, and neither of us ever turned down a chance to put one of them in the ice chest.

Charlie adjusted the trolling speed to keep the ballyhoo baits just barely skipping as I put the two rods in the rod holder. We trolled with Penn 4/0 reels and 50-pound test line, not because the dolphins were that big, but because in the blue water, you never know what kind of fish may be waiting below.

A short time later, as we talked about the lack of weeds and wondered if we would even see a dolphin, it happened. Seemingly out of nowhere, a huge bull dolphin came leaping out of the water off our port bow. He was running full speed, a streaky blur of yellow and green just under the surface as he headed for our two baits.

Out of the water one more time, he came down on one of the ballyhoos and began stripping line from the reel. If you have never seen a dolphin crash a bait spread, you have missed perhaps the most exciting, blood-rushing experience in fishing. A 50-pound fish moving at what seemed to be 50 miles an hour had just about broken the butt off the rod in the rod holder as he ran away from the boat.

Charlie ran the boat, and I fought the fish. Several jumps and runs later, we had him at the boat. I say we had him. We had him on the end of the line, but we also had more dolphin than I had ever seen before, under the boat.

As Charlie put the boat in neutral and I continued to move my fish closer to the boat, Charlie grabbed a spinning rod, one that had been pre-rigged with a double line and a bare hook, and added a chunk of ballyhoo to the hook. He tossed it to the side of the boat and immediately hooked up.

He placed his spinning rod in a rod holder and in one swift, continuous motion gaffed my fish and dropped him in the fish box. As my fish banged around in the fish box, Charlie handed me a spinning rod, and I followed his earlier lead and hooked up again. While I fought my second fish, Charlie boated his first and then hooked up again.

Dolphins are peculiar fish in one respect. They generally won't leave a brother fish. If you keep a hooked fish in the water next to the boat, the entire school will usually remain around the boat.

We continued to double-team fish in this manner for about 15 minutes, boating about ten dolphins in the 5- to 10-pound range. I could look beneath the boat at any point in time and see dolphin everywhere down to about a 70-foot depth. The water was that clear.

It was as if someone turned off a light switch. I looked over the side as I boated a fish and saw dolphin everywhere. Only seconds later, they had disappeared. As Charlie and I puzzled over the swift departure of fish, the reason for their departure came into view.

I have seen some big sharks in my day; I've even caught quite a few. But this bad boy was one of the biggest I had ever seen. A hammerhead that appeared to be as long as our 20-foot boat slowly swam beneath us. Then another one appeared, and before long we had an entire school of hammerheads at varying depths under the boat.

They were fascinating to watch, and as sharks go, appeared to be quite agile in the water. Their small eyes were placed one on each end of their hammer-like heads. I remembered the times that my father would catch a small one several times over and would, out of frustration, carve the two hammer appendages off like he was whittling a piece of wood, leaving a sightless bleeding shark to swim away. And then suddenly as quickly as they appeared, they disappeared into the deep blue.

We never got up with that school of dolphin again that day. But we did have fish, and we even ended up catching a small blackfin tuna. He hit a skipped ballyhoo.

But, probably more important than the fish that day, though, was another chance to fish with Charlie and record yet another memory of a great fishing adventure.

Charlie. Every angler should have a Charlie in their life.

Finger Lickin' Chicken Fish AKA Yellowtail

This one is as true as they get and yet still a bit unbelievable…

It was in April some 30 years ago, somewhere around Easter that we made a two-day trip to Marquesas Keys off Key West. We took two boats for safety, and after the five-hour drive from Miami, we launched at Stock Island Marina. Six of us went this time, two in my 20-foot SeaCraft and the others in a 26-foot Ana Capri.

The weather this time of year can be very unpredictable, warm, even hot, one day and cold the next. This particular day and the days that followed were not the best. A high, scuddy sky and wind threatened that kind of slow drizzle that makes for miserable fishing. But, off we went anyway for the 26-mile trip, trying to stay dry both from the rain and from the bow spray.

Marquesas Key is the only true atoll in the Atlantic, sort of a doughnut of mangroves perched on a shallow coral reef. The hole in the doughnut is probably a quarter mile in diameter with several meandering channels cutting across the 2-foot deep water from one side to the other. Our plan was to anchor up in one of these small channels at night under the protection of the mangroves. That first morning was spent trying to locate some fish. Our sister boat headed for the Gulf of Mexico side while we trolled the edge of the reef line on the Atlantic side. It was a little too early in the year for dolphin and a little too late for kingfish, so we located and anchored up from a school of yellowtail snapper on the edge of the reef holding on a hump in 90 feet of water.

About 30 minutes of chumming with sand balls (ground up fish mixed with beach sand) was all it took to get things started. Weightless chunks of bait on 3/0 hooks drifting back into the chum line would hook up a yellowtail almost every time.

By now we were hungry and had caught quite a number of yellowtail. We shared a couple of boxes of frozen fried chicken that we had allowed to thaw in the midmorning air. The chicken was cold but good. We continued fishing and eating and throwing the chicken bones over the side, still catching fish.

It was at about that point we began catching fish with bulging stomachs (the fish's, not ours!). They looked distorted, so much so that we had to cut one open to see what was going on. There, inside the stomach of a 15-inch yellowtail, was a 6-inch long leg bone from a chicken! He had swallowed the whole thing (or is it the thing whole?)! Neither of us could believe our eyes! We continued to catch fish there until our chum and chicken ran out, and then ran back to the island to set up for the night.

The next morning we made a run to Ellis Rock on the Gulf side with our sister boat. But the swells had gotten larger, and neither of our stomachs fares well in rough water, so we came back. At the island, we tried to idle across the doughnut, but the tide was too low, and we were kicking up mud everywhere. My partner, Sam, from North Carolina, had no idea what was going on in that shallow water, but I knew exactly what I wanted to do.

We got out of the boat to lighten the load and float it a little higher. Then we pushed and pulled the boat across the hole in the doughnut toward the lee side mangroves. As I had suspected, about 10 yards from the edge of the mangrove limbs, the water dropped off from 1 foot to about 8 or 10 feet deep, going back under the trees. Sam did not see what I saw, and he could not figure why we were in 2 feet of water next to the mangroves.

I told Sam to follow my lead and tied on a white with red wrapping, 2-inch nylon jig (one of my grandfather's handmade jigs), tipped with a small strip of mullet. I told Sam to throw carefully at a dead branch on one of the trees and work the jig slowly. He did, and a mangrove snapper with fire in his eyes came from under the mangroves. It took Sam's jig back under the tree with him. Sam could not believe it! Pound for pound, these things fight better than any fish you will ever catch! They weren't huge, but they were plentiful, and we fished until we ran out of bait and jigs.

Back at Stock Island late that afternoon, preparing for the drive back, we kept what fish we wanted to eat and sold the remainder of our catch. Fish houses always had a truck there in the afternoon to buy fish.

To this day, no one believes the yellowtail and chicken bones, or at least they accept it with a wink. I haven't been back to the Key West area in quite some years, but my guess is that those mangrove snappers are still there under the mangroves. I would also guess that the yellowtail still school over the deep humps. But given our situation today, we probably could not catch them. See, after all these years and at my age, my chicken is grilled with no bones!

'Dance with the One What Brung Ya'

Fish for what's biting!

Someone asked me the other day - what's your favorite fish? I thought for a minute and named a species, snapper as I recall. But I thought about that encounter later and began pondering about just what my favorite fish is.

I grew up with a rod and reel in my hand. I fished fresh water, saltwater, and all water in between for just about every species I can think of as I write this.

I certainly liked fishing for bass in the Everglades and canals of South Florida. Trips to Lake Okeechobee were few and far between for a kid my age, and I looked on those as if they were trips to a holy shrine. Bass and panfish angling is relatively easy and can be done with little expense. Every pond or body of water has fish, and they are readily accessible.

For a kid growing up in Key West and South Florida, I had the best of both worlds. A short walk or bike ride from my house on Pine Street in Key West put me at the water's edge. Yes, Elizabeth, we had bicycles back then!

A short walk or bike ride from my house in South Miami put me either at the water's edge on Biscayne Bay or at one of the myriad canals that crisscross the landscape there. All of those canals had fish – they still do. Today you can even catch the exotic peacock bass imported from South America.

My favorite fish became the black bass at that point. As I grew and obtained wheels – my first car was a '52 Plymouth I bought from my uncle for $75 – I was able to reach a little farther with my rod.

On any given Friday night I would hit every accessible canal from Homestead to Key Biscayne in search of snook. Catching snook became almost an obsession when I was in high school. I had a rod and tackle in the car, and before I did anything else after school, I was on the bank of Snapper Creek chunking a white bucktail. Much to the detriment of my grades, I would spend the entire afternoon catching and releasing snook, tarpon and jack crevalle at the mouth of that canal where it ran into Biscayne Bay. My fishing buddies and I caught a ton of fish like that, although I was perfectly happy to be there alone.

They say you are a true angler when you can catch a trophy fish while no one else is around and release it to fight another day. I must be a true angler, because I have done that more than once. Some anglers fish all their lives in search of a trophy black bass – a "10 pounder" to put on the wall. I can truthfully say I am lucky enough to have released more than one like that while fishing alone over the years.

Fishing with my father put a whole new perspective on things. He was a meat fisherman. If the fish he caught wasn't very good to eat, it was a "trash" fish and not worth catching. I can remember numerous times he hooked a huge tarpon – I'm talking in the 150-pound range – and then did everything he could to break the fish off so he could catch something worth keeping. Some of my friends who read this column knew him and can attest to his habits.

Before Chef Paul Prudhomme took a lowly redfish and blackened it in a skillet many years back, no one targeted reds, and they could be caught everywhere. I have been with my father more times than I can remember when a school of reds began biting along a channel cut, and we would crank up and leave, so we didn't waste all our live bait. We could probably have caught a hundred fish in that one spot – but they were trash fish to him.

I remember fishing one day with my father and uncle. We were drifting across Rocky Channel out of Flamingo looking for seatrout. All three of us simultaneously hooked up to fighting freight trains. These were three bull reds, all of them around 30 pounds. When my father saw what they were, I had to beg and plead with him to let at least me finish catching the fish. We all three did that and lifted them together. What I would have given for a camera on that trip.

Speaking of cameras, it always seemed that we only took pictures after the fact – when we got home.

I think the biggest fish I ever caught would have to be a shark. Not my favorite fish… I never really kept track, but I know we brought many sharks alongside to cut the leader, and these fish were as long as our boat and almost as wide. I hooked a hammerhead one time while dolphin fishing that made me cut the line long before he got close to the boat. He was big enough to overturn our 20-foot SeaCraft and never miss a beat. But, you see, these sharks were trash fish to us.

The biggest "eating" fish was and still is the 347-pound Goliath grouper (jewfish) that my father and I caught. Remember our camera situation? We had to talk a tourist who happened to be at the marina at Flamingo into taking our picture. Then we gave him some money and our address. Several weeks later, the picture of us with that fish came in the mail.

In all of this - biggest, best eating, hardest fighting – one thing stands out. All kinds of fish held a favorite status at some point in my life. Bass, snapper, jewfish, dolphin, crappie, grouper, kingfish, flounder, redfish, trout, and more all hold a special place in my world. So the question regarding my favorite fish necessarily has to be qualified by a time frame.

I will tell you what had happened over time, however. After bringing up my sons and teaching them to fish – yes, my daughter as well – I have found a real joy in simply being able to fish. I have grandchildren now getting old enough to fish with me, and although my back can't take the all-day strain it once could, I'll be there with fishing with them as well.

And while I do that and think back on just what my favorite fish is, I believe I have found the answer. It's quite simple really. My favorite fish is the one that is currently hooked and pulling my string. I was somehow good enough to entice him to bite - and I do so love catching most any fish - that I have to give this one the current honor. Someone once told me to "dance with the one what brung ya." So I'll do just that and be very happy to catch the fish that took my bait – the one that is right now my favorite fish.

Dunnaway's Bones

Vic Dunnaway was the outdoor editor of the old Miami Daily News back in the day. We read his articles every Thursday and then went out to try what he suggested...

We were two high school boys, looking for a place to catch fish. A 12-foot wooden skiff was perched upside down on top of the old 1952 Plymouth as we drove across the causeway to Key Biscayne. We had no car top carrier, and if we turned too abruptly, the boat shifted, causing us to stop to reposition it. The top of the old car showed the signs of several fishing trips.

Mashta Point was, and still is, at the south end of Key Biscayne. Undeveloped back then, it was a favorite spot for bank-fishermen and provided an ideal launching place for our small boat. As we unloaded the boat, some anglers watched with envy. As small as it was, it was still a boat, something the other anglers did not have.

The boat was originally 12 feet long. My dad found it on the side of the road somewhere and brought it home by sitting it inside his boat. The transom was rotted out, which was obviously the reason it had been discarded. We spent a week or so cutting the aft 2 feet off the boat and replacing the transom. While I did that, Pop somehow acquired an old Wizard 6-horse air-cooled engine. The only thing good about the engine was that it ran – at least in the barrel behind the house.

With everything in the boat, we sputtered out of the small inlet and headed for the finger channels to the south. The boat moved at snail's pace, a little more than 5 knots.

Five minutes into the journey, we had to stop and anchor the boat. We had not reached our fishing spot; we simply had to stop every five minutes to let the motor cool off. It wasn't by choice; the motor shut down because it overheated. It was a fact we took in stride. Several overheat stops later, we eased onto the shoal and grass flat that marks the north end of the finger channels.

Stiltsville. The name is very descriptive. Houses on stilts or pilings dotted the flats. Some of them were quite elaborate, owned by families with money. Some of them were basic fishing cabins, built many years before as a weekend fishing haunt. We were glad they were there. On more than one occasion, we had to ask for a tow back to Mashta Point.

On the flats in the gin clear water, you could see fish moving. You had to be good to distinguish the movement, but the fish were there. At low tide, as the current slowed on the change, we searched for tails. Bonefish were abundant on all of these flats. We never really fished much for them, because we were brought up as meat fishermen. That is, we need to bring fish home to eat, and no one eats a bonefish.

Tails. This time, we were looking for tails. We had read Vic Dunnaway's Thursday Fishing column in the Miami Herald. Memory says the Herald, but it could have been the Daily News. Either way, he talked about bonefish on the flats. Back then, whatever Vic said in the paper became the gospel as far as we were concerned. If he told us that fish were moving up the drainage pipes from Biscayne Bay, we would probably be found fishing in the drain on the corner of Miami Avenue and Flagler Street! To us he was the supreme source of fishing knowledge. As we scanned the water, we saw some tails. Some tails? I would guess there were no less than 50 in every direction we looked.

A Hurricane rod, an Orvis 100 spinning reel, and a small white bucktail were our standard equipment. If it couldn't be caught on a white bucktail, we figured it wasn't worth catching.

We both began chunking our bucktails across the flat. There was no precise presentation, no slipping the lure into the water ahead of the fish. It was cast and retrieve, and it was cast in every direction.

My guess is we caught more than 30 bonefish that morning without moving from one spot. Some of them were quite large as memory serves. We were using 6- or 8-pound test line and these bones would strip most of it off our reel before we could turn them.

We had no net; we used no leader. Technique was not our strong point. We never cranked to run down a fish. But catch fish we did.

I remember that day well, but I was never really that impressed by the bonefish we caught. I never understood the big deal about catching a bonefish! Heck, I could go out there almost any time and catch one. But, what good was it? You couldn't eat it!

What I remember most about that trip was what we did after we tired of catching bones. We moved to the edge of a favorite finger channel and caught snapper. As I remember it, we ended up with a couple of mangrove snapper in the 5-pound range, several smaller lane snapper, and one mutton snapper.

We caught a ton of bones that morning, and relatively few snapper that afternoon. But, it was the snapper that made our day, because we brought fish home to eat. Isn't it amazing how one's perspective on life and life's activities can change the measure of one's success?

I'm sure the bones still patrol those flats south of Key Biscayne, though probably fewer in number and far more wary. I have a whole different appreciation for them since those days. Placing a shrimp fly in the right spot ahead of a tailing bone is no easy feat. And turning a screaming bone on a five weight with 4-pound tippet makes my heart pound!

Much as I wish I could fish as we did back then I know you can't go back. I guess my perspective on life has changed.

Born with a Silver Hook...

A silver spoon would have been nice – I could have afforded a whole lot bigger boat...

The well-known idiom about being born with a silver spoon in one's mouth had a bearing on this piece. That spoon, representing wealth and the never-ending supply of things that wealth brings, turned out to be a fish hook in my case.

From a father who taught me to fish and seldom went without me at his side, to a nonfishing wife who has graciously endured the past 40 years alongside me, to my children, all of whom have acquired at least some portion of that same hook, my life has revolved around fishing.

Wherever we lived, I somehow found a place to fish. It didn't matter whether it was a freshwater neighborhood retention pond or the banks of the Intracoastal Waterway in North Carolina, I always found a way to fish.

Every time we moved, and we moved 11 times at the instance of my day job, I always looked for a home on or close to the water. I wanted my children to be able to find places to fish as I did at their age.

Whether it was a silver hook or just my heavy-handed guidance, it worked. Both of my sons enjoy fishing as much as I did. My daughter enjoys fishing as well, although she is very much like her mother – they both prefer the catching aspect.

It is with this silver hook, with this drive to fish that I put together these tales, all of them true, all of them giving a glimpse of some aspect of my life.

With the smell of hot lard sizzling in a skillet filling the air, I watched my father scaling hand-sized bluegill at the water's edge. The skillet was propped up by a ring of coral rocks, sitting on a smoky fire of Australian pine wood, made ever smokier by the pine needles.

The wind made a particular sound moving through these pines, and their pine needles made a carpet of soft brown, covering the rocks and preventing weeds from growing. And on the wind was the smell of everglades muck – that jet-black dirt that formed the 6- to 12-inch growing layer on top of the coral rock bed.

This is my first recollection of fishing – the sights, the sounds, the smells. It would be repeated many times, with varying numbers of people – aunts, uncles, cousins, but always with our family.

This was the Tamiami Trail in 1950, U.S. 41 west out of Miami. Back then, the two-lane road had no side rails, and the canal that resulted from digging the fill to make the road ran parallel to it the entire distance to the west side of Florida. Cars would pull off in between the Australian pines that lined the "trail" most of the way across the state.

Seminole Indians (actually Miccosukee, but we never knew them by any other name than Seminole) lived along the other side of the canal in small villages. The men wore jeans and a colorful shirt they called a "big shirt." The older women wore the traditional and distinctive patchwork dresses. They lived in and under the palmetto thatch-roofed huts and used a small boat to cross the canal where they might have a truck or car parked. I never could figure out how the old cars that I would occasionally see on the other side of the canal next to their huts got there.

The "40-mile bend" was a special place in my mind for many years. It was a place talked about by my father and other grown-ups as if it were some Promised Land of fishing. It was 40 miles west of Miami, and there was nothing between Miami and the bend but a few Indian camps, and nothing beyond the bend but the road to Everglades City and Chokoloskee on the West Coast. You needed a full tank of gas, good tires, and a dependable vehicle to make the trip to the bend.

Dixie Webb had a place at the bend. We only went there once, because my father was fearful of the "characters" that frequented the place. Many years later I would go there as an adult, while Mr. Webb was still alive and enjoyed some of the best breakfasts I ever ate – country ham and grits cooked in pure cream instead of water.

If all this sounds like a story, it is. But, it's a true story of how I grew up fishing – how I was born with a silver hook in my mouth.

Trolling a Creek for Tarpon and Snook

Since this piece came out, I have received numerous emails telling about other anglers who troll for tarpon...

Mention tarpon fishing and visions of fly rods and saltwater, flats skiffs come to most people's mind. No one ever thinks about trolling when you mention tarpon, at least no one with any sense. If you've read many of my past features, you will know that sometimes my fishing exploits are a little different!

On the southwest tip of Florida, just north of Cape Sable, is a small saltwater mangrove creek named Turner Creek. It meanders back into the land of mangroves and mud flats for about 2 miles before it opens to a huge open area, too shallow to navigate. This is one of the creeks in which we fished for jewfish with Calcutta cane poles. This open flat is covered with wonderful bird life at low tide - spoonbills, egrets, herons, and all manner of wading birds walking the mud flat in search of food.

Fishing for jewfish meant waiting for a high slack tide. We arrived about an hour early this day, and for lack of anything else to do, we idled back in the creek to see just how far we could go. To this day I can't remember why we decided to put a line out, or which of us came up with the idea. But somehow a white bucktail jig ended up out the back of the boat as we moved up the creek.

Before we moved more than 100 yards, a tarpon jumped on the bucktail. He was small, about 10 pounds, but he thought he was a lot bigger! Two jumps later, the jig came flying back in our direction. Figuring there had to be more, we turned around and headed back the way we came. In a few minutes, we had another tarpon hooked. This one stayed hooked, but as he took line and headed around the bend, we lost him in the mangrove tangle. The winding creek didn't leave a lot of room for fish fighting.

We spent the next hour or so trolling up and down the creek, catching ten small tarpons and two snook, and losing probably twice that many. We tried stopping and casting a variety of lures, but for some reason, the fish preferred the trolled bucktail bait to one being retrieved from a cast. It was an amazing day!

Turner Creek is still there, a part of Everglades National Park, but not fishable any longer. Boat traffic has been stopped in the creek by the National Park Service because this particular estuary creek is a nesting area for the saltwater crocodile. But the fish must still be there! I never caught another tarpon or snook trolling, but then again, I don't think I ever trolled for them again!

Catching Redfish on a Fly

This trip was another one for the story books. But it did happen, and we really did catch the fish...

I never was much of a fly fisherman - never really took the time to learn, early on. It's like a lot of other things in life where you just sort of learn as you go out of necessity. Like, the best way to get cold, hard butter onto a piece of hot toast is obviously to pick the stick of butter up and use it as a giant yellow crayon. Hey, it worked for me, even if my mother did banish me from the kitchen forever!

Well, so it was for my fly-fishing education. I had the hardest time figuring out how that thick line was going to fit through the eye of that tiny hook! And when I noticed other people using some monofilament leader, the problem turned to the size of the barrel knot I used to link the two lines together! Live and learn, as they say, although my learning comes the hard way, a fact that my wife has thankfully endured for over 30 years.

We were up the creek without a paddle, as the saying goes, on this particular day. It was a matter of not having enough water under the boat to float it because it had all mysteriously disappeared - just ran out from under the boat, leaving us to remember just how low the tide can get on a midfall day (another learning experience!). My partner, Jim, and I had purposely waited for the outgoing tide, planning to find redfish retreating from their foraging on the grass and mud flats off the Intracoastal Waterway. In all the commotion of catching fish, we never realized how low the tide had gotten until it was too late!

So here we are, catching fish and unable to move the boat. The outside bends in the creek still held upward of 6 feet of water, but it quickly shallowed to a foot or less as the creek wound to the next bend. Redfish were everywhere, coming off the flats in droves and dropping into the deeper holes. They weren't swimming hard, merely staying in line and letting the current take them. Schools of 15 or 20 of them would scurry across the thin water between deep holes, bulging a wake before them. Nosing a little mud here, and flipping an oyster shell there, they occasionally came upon a small crab. You could tell when that happened because they dropped into a lower gear and spurted for the short chase and ensuing meal. It's easy to get enthralled as you watch something like this happen. Maybe twice before in my life have I been able to witness so many fish in the wild doing what the books say they do!

We had stopped fishing and started watching the reds coming from the flat. Four here, then five more, then another four over there - it was beautiful. While all this was taking place, Jim started fiddling around in the rod box and came up with a fly rod. I say fly rod because that is what it resembled, not because it was in any condition to be used. It was the one I had owned from my pre-teen years, the one I went to school on. I had no idea that it was still around, let alone in the boat. Tells you how often I clean the boat - but that's another story!

We had been catching reds on jigs and grubs; some tipped with mud minnows, some tipped with shrimp. We went for a long time where every cast resulted in a hookup - Jim with a fish, me with an oyster bar! But we soon realized that these fish would hit the grubs without the extra bait tip. This fact is what drove Jim to do what he did, and it has become known between the two of us as "the day."

Taking a plain, straight 3/0 hook, Jim simply threaded a chartreuse swim-tail grub on the hook, and then tied this on the end of some very old tippet. Several hauls later, the grub landed rather rudely in front of a nice single red coming off the flat. As it drifted with and in front of the fish, it looked pretty appealing with the swimming action of the tail. That redfish wasted no time inhaling the grub. I'm not sure who was more surprised, me, the fish or Jim, who now found himself tied to the business end of a 20-pound redfish.

The first few seconds were thrilling as the rod doubled over and the line began streaking from the reel. We both cheered as we watched that bull rip across the shallow water from our bend in the creek toward the next bend in the creek. I think it was at about that point that we both realized that Jim needed to stop this fish and turn him before he reached the next bend. "No problem," we both said, "That tippet has to be at least ten years old." Just hold the reel, and it will break. The only problem was, no one told the line it was supposed to break. The fish kept running, the line kept leaving, and Jim started yelling!

The fish made it to the next bend and, to our amazement continued downstream. If I stood on the bow of the boat, I could see the snake pattern of the creek as it twisted left and right, sometimes turning back on itself like a hairpin. As Jim stood on the bow, he could see the wake of his fish over the stretch of marsh grass now moving from left to right in front of him, one turn in the creek away.

As the fish made it to the next bend, we both said enough is enough. Just crank down on the reel, point the rod at the fish and let him have the grub and old leader. So Jim did just that. And the line tightened, almost singing in the breeze. But the fish continued left to right, and the line did not break. The fish turned toward the next hole away from Jim. And the line still did not break. But as the fish turned and again tried to run directly away from Jim, it rolled and turned back. Jim had turned him! But now what?

Jim had a 20-pound redfish turned, two creek bends away and across the grass - and on an old rod with a rotten line that refused to break. Knowing we could never get to the fish, we began to handline him. Obviously on the backing, we began to drag the fish toward the bank of the creek, trying to break the line. Surely the tippet would break under enough strain, we thought. But on this day we would have to think again. Not only did the line not break, it appeared that it was strong enough to drag the fish up into the marsh grass. And so began a debate on the relative merits of attempting to drag the fish across the marsh, versus simply letting it continue to swim in the creek next to the grass. By this time, the concern was for the fish and making sure that we could somehow release him. Do we wade over and attempt to traverse the marsh grass to get to him? Do we wait for the tide to come in and float the boat?

The marsh grass route was quickly dispatched. That grass is growing in waist deep mud, and we would never get through it. Waiting for the tide was an option, but we figured it would be about two hours before we had enough water to float. It was then that we decided on what turned out to be the idea of the day. Well, it was good in theory.

How do you float a boat in the very shallow water? Take the weight out of it. So Jim and I both slipped over the side of the boat, Jim with the fly rod and I with the anchor rope. The boat did come up a little bit, but it still was wedged in the sand/mud/oyster shell bottom.

A few heaves and shoves got the boat into the deeper part of the creek, and it appeared that our plan might work! Excitedly, we began trudging down the creek toward the bend, with the boat half floating and half sliding across the bottom and shallow water. Thirty minutes, several slips, multiple oyster shell cuts, and lots of sweat later, we had the boat at the bend in the creek. Around the bend we went, dragging, grunting and bleeding, headed for the fish - oh yes, remember the fish? While we were making every effort to get to him, he was calmly swimming around in that part of the creek. It was almost as if he knew what we were doing.

Jim left me behind pulling the boat and began wading the shallow water toward the fish. Amazingly, the fish did not make a run. A few short spurts and a couple of head shakes later, and the fish was at Jim's feet. As Jim bent down and grabbed the leader to release the fish, the leader broke! The fish sat there for a few seconds, and then calmly moved off with the tide, bulging a wake ahead of him, a chartreuse grub on the side of his mouth. Jim and I just stood there and watched, and then looked at each other and grinned. We both had the same feeling of accomplishment. Standing there muddy, bleeding and sore, we both knew we would have done it again.

I've caught a lot of fish on a fly since then, a lot of redfish, in fact, a lot of them on that same old rod in that same creek. But none of them match the thrill of that one day when Jim decided to catch a redfish on an old fly rod!

Fiddling for Crabs

Repeat after me: Catching bait can be fun. Catching bait can be fun. Catching bait can be fun...

Sometimes the best-laid plans don't work out as well as I would like. As well as I would like? Heck, sometimes they fall apart right before my very eyes!

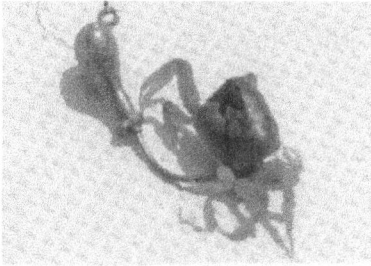

John was tired of paying those high prices for bait, and so was I. They weren't that high, but we didn't have the money at the time to afford what we needed. Between fishing and family, money was thin and we tried to scrimp and save.

So it was that we devised a way to catch our bait this particular day. We drew up plans and constructed a method that we had both heard about but never attempted. We were going to catch our weight in fiddler crabs! Yes, those little sideways running dudes that roam the sandy flats at low tide were prime bait at this time of year. The sheepshead bite was on, and fiddlers were like a steak dinner to them.

The plan went something like this: At low tide, while all the crabs are running around on the wet sand, we would dig a hole in the sand about 2 feet deep. Simple enough so far. Next, we would take several one by four boards and form a "V" in the sand with the fulcrum of the "V" being the hole we dug. The boards would be set on their side, making a little fence on each side that ended at the hole in the sand. We figured one 8-foot board on each side would do the trick. The idea here is to herd the crabs into the funnel and ultimately into the hole in the sand! Simple, huh?

We hit the beach as the tide approached its low ebb and began looking for fiddlers. To our supreme satisfaction, they were everywhere! They were out roaming and eating, jumping in a close hole as any seagulls flew their way. Seagulls will willingly eat fiddlers, but even with as many crabs as we saw on the beach, we did not see the birds diving at them. We were both puzzled, but hey, what the heck, the crabs are here and so are we, so let's catch some bait!

First-order of business? Dig the hole! Remember those great plans? No shovel! After a "you do it," "no, you do it" discussion that lasted 15 minutes, I got down on my hands and knees and began digging the hole – no shovel, mind you, just bare hands.

It quickly became apparent that this hole was a bigger chore than we thought. First of all, it began filling with water coming up through the sand. Secondly, the water tended to wash around and slope the sides of the hole. We needed a vertical side that would prevent anything from crawling out of the hole! We settled for what we had and went after the boards.

We wedged the boards into the sand and made a pretty good fence for each side of the "V." Everything was set. Nothing to do now but herd the crabs!

Remember the TV commercial that came on during the Super Bowl that talked about herding cats? Keep that picture in your head.

As we approached the crabs, John started running out and around one way, and I started running the other way. Picture two nuts running around in the sand chasing crabs! We found out that they would do one of two things. If we walked slowly, they would simply move away slowly. If we ran or walked fast, they would dive into the first available hole. So here we go, each of us walking slowly toward the open end of the "V" with crabs moving ahead of us. This is where problem No. 2 popped up.

We had to walk so slowly that the crabs would completely avoid moving inside the "V." Aha! We need a couple more boards to make the "V" wider! Off to the truck went John. Back with some boards, he made the "V" wider and we began again. This is where problem three popped up.

We found out how easily these little crabs, not much bigger than a quarter, can climb over a 4-inch board. We are now two hours into this ordeal, and the tide is coming in!

So we put our heads together and studied the situation. While we talked, it was as if they were all listening to us and watching us. We began talking in whispers as if they could hear us! But the plan was this - we would slowly herd them away from the boards and then rush back and close all the holes anywhere in front of the boards. Then we could run at them, and they had no place to go except between the boards. And so it was that John and I closed all the holes. We walked far from the boards, and began running in a zigzag fashion, whooping and hollering to get the crabs herded into the hole. And, do you know, it worked! We had a hole full of wet swimming crabs! This is where problem No. 4 popped up.

I told John to put the bucket in the truck. He swears he did that and that it must have blown out – but either way, we still had no bucket for the crabs. So with the crabs relatively calm and safe in the hole, we both head back up to the road to find something to hold the crabs. This is where the final straw was placed on the proverbial camel's back.

"I've been watching you fellas for a while now," he said. "You guys look kind of silly running around out there. Just what is it you were doing?" The "he" in this exchange was the state park ranger, and "he" was parked right behind our truck on the side of the road.

"Oh we're catching bait – fiddlers – and we got a hole full of them," I said. "We just need something to put them in and we will be all set."

The ranger was so nice, and he offered a cardboard box he had in his trunk. What a deal! We said thanks and started to head back to the crabs when he said, "Oh, one more thing."

As he handed us a long yellow piece of paper, he said, "The court date is next month, so you'll have time to use your bait. But next time, boys, you need to park somewhere else."

I looked at the paper – a traffic violation in a state park – and then looked up at my truck. We had parked right in front of the no parking sign. Neither of us even saw it when we first arrived. I walked over to it to see if it had been freshly placed, but alas, it was there long before we were!

We got our crabs and caught our sheepshead. By the time we finished paying the parking fine, those crabs cost us about $50 for an eight-ounce cupful. The bait shop across the street sells them for $3.

Damn the Torpedoes...

Now and then something happens to a boater that makes us laugh as we watch a comedy of errors. It's a lot different when people are laughing at you instead...

One day on the water can make a man feel like he is on top of the world – or not! I fished with my friend Bill, who had just bought a new engine for his boat. Now understand that this new engine was being mounted on a 20-year-old boat, and that the transom of this boat was in such bad shape that the dealer selling the engine refused to mount it. He also refused to honor any warranty on it if someone else mounted it.

Unfazed by these non-veiled threats, Bill bought the engine anyway.

How did that famous WWII quote go, "Damn the torpedoes, full speed ahead"?

The transom on this old fiberglass boat was mushy. That means you could push in on it and it would bend and give. In police work, they call that a clue. The wood inside that fiberglass was rotten. Today's boats use a solid or composite transom material that is impervious to rot. Thirty years ago, most transoms and stringers in a fiberglass boat were still made of wood. Once the water got to that wood, the rotting process began. They call it "dry rot" for some reason, but it has always been wet and damp on any that I tried to repair.

On our trip, we had to drive about 70 miles to reach the ramp where we planned to launch. The trailer on this rig was probably in worse shape than the boat itself – rusty and ragged.

About 20 miles into the trip we had our first problem, a flat tire on the old trailer. This was no ordinary flat tire; this was a tire coming completely off the rim. Luckily, we were close to one of those big, box stores that sell everything under the sun. A short time later we had purchased and mounted a new tire and rim, and we were on our way again

Damn the torpedoes…

Why we didn't think about the other trailer tire is beyond me, but suffice it to say, we didn't. As it turned out, the other tire held up all the way to the boat ramp.

Launching the boat is usually quite easy. We were at a big, wide ramp, one capable of handling eight to 10 launches simultaneously. The flat tire had put us behind in on our schedule, and we were there with some other boaters – lots of people watching each other.

My father had a peculiar hobby when he retired. He would take a lawn chair and a cooler and go to the local public boat ramp on a Saturday morning, and watch the launching circus. I say circus, because weekend boaters usually include first-timers, and the launching sequence can produce some really funny situations. Had he been at this ramp on this morning, he would have been laughing.

We backed the boat down until the water reached the bottom edge of the tire rims on the trailer. This was pretty standard on a trailer that old. Not many float-on trailers were in use when this one was built. The idea was to keep the saltwater off the wheel bearings. This trailer had rollers, and the procedure was to actually "launch" the boat off the trailer, allowing it to roll down into the water. Only, the boat would not budge.

We figured that the rollers must have been frozen and would not turn. So we went to the front of the trailer, put our shoulders on each side of the bow, and began to heave. The bow lifted off the trailer, but the boat would not move. We heaved again – the boat still refused to move. We asked a neighboring launcher to help heave – the boat still refused to move.

Now we had four or five men standing in front of the trailer, all offering suggestions. The best suggestion, we thought, was to back the trailer into the water a little farther and let the transom float up. That would surely free the sticking boat. We failed to see the torpedo that was heading straight for us again.

Bill got in the truck and backed the trailer down farther into the water. I waved him back as I watched the back of the boat, waiting for it to float up off the trailer. But, by the time I finally realized that it was not floating up, the top of the transom was underwater, and the boat was quickly filling.

I yelled for him to stop and pull the boat back up, but by this time the rear tires on the truck had reached that mossy, slippery part of the boat ramp – that one that so many people slip on at low tide.

Our crew of advisors had been depleted by now – they had launched and left. New advisors were watching, and I yelled to ask them for some help. Some sat on the back of the truck to put more weight on the rear axle. Some pushed. In short order we had the boat – now half full of water – up on the ramp.

It was about then that our advisors began to smile and chuckle (they had to be dying laughing on the inside). Firmly attached to the boat's transom was the tie-down strap (aka torpedo) we had forgotten to remove.

Embarrassed, we finally got the boat drained of seawater and launched it. It launched quite easily once we removed that torpedo.

A run of about 10 miles across Florida Bay was ahead of us. No worries – we had a brand-new engine. It ran quite well, and we headed out to fish. It turned out to be a good fishing trip as far as fishing went. We caught a box full of trout and snappers.

On the way back in, the afternoon sea breeze had kicked up, and we were bouncing in a 3-foot chop. About half way in, I turned to see our wake and watch the flats around us. I caught the movement out of the corner of my eye – another torpedo had been launched at us. But this time luck was with us. As we quartered the oncoming waves, the boat rolled back and forth in those waves. The movement I caught was that of the new engine. It was wobbling back and forth, left and right on the transom!

I yelled, and we stopped the boat. I went to the stern and saw that the engine had two hand tightening knobs holding it on the transom. Had the dealer mounted it, he would have drilled and bolted it down. Since Bill mounted it himself, he figured that the hand knobs would do just fine.

They had loosened, and it was sheer luck that we caught it before the engine came off the transom. I began tightening the knobs; only they would not tighten. Oh, they screwed in all right – into the transom – but nothing got tight. They actually had broken through the fiberglass on the transom and were mushing through that rotten wood.

Suffice it to say; we idled the rest of the way back to the ramp. Once on the trailer, we found that the engine was so unstable that we had to lift it off the boat, disconnect all the wiring, and put it in the back of the truck.

Bill began the day on top of the world - new (to him) boat; new engine; and, a day of fishing. He ended it with several torpedo holes in him and in his boat.

Once we got the boat on the trailer, he asked me to drive home. He said he didn't feel well for some reason.

It was a tedious ride home. It would have made a better story had that other tire blown – a final torpedo. But the old tire held, and we made it back safely.

The boat? It got repaired – he had a new transom put in it, and had the engine professionally mounted – this time with bolts. And he still uses it today. I believe I can safely say that he now goes fishing and does feel on top of the world!

Be Ready for the Unexpected

Sometimes fishing brings about a situation that makes you wish you had done something different...

Always expect the unexpected. Now if that isn't the silliest statement I ever heard! Heck if you expect everything, nothing is unexpected! Are you confused? Imagine how confused I was when a jewfish about 90 pounds or so came rolling up on the end of my 6-pound-test line!

It had been one of those days we all have, where you just could not buy a bite. We were in Whitewater Bay around marker 36, drifting for seatrout with popping corks and live shrimp. Fishing was simply terrible, with the hot sun, almost no wind to aid our drift, and, of course, no fish.

Whitewater is a pristine estuary, arguably the largest inland breeding grounds for a variety of saltwater fish. Located at the southwest tip of Florida, it is a maze of mangrove islands, creeks, cuts and open water. Those who are new to the area are ill advised to venture too far off the markers because, after a couple of turns around some islands, everything looks the same.

To get out of the sun, and eat a sandwich or two, we idled around to the back of a mangrove island and tied up under an overhanging branch. The relief from the sun was a welcome change, and it allowed us to cool off and relax.

We set a couple of rods out on the bottom with a shrimp and cut mullet. As we ate, we could see the telltale slow pecks of a crab on our bait. Slowly, we would reel in the bait, with the very stubborn crab hanging on to its newfound meal. A quick dip of a net and we had ourselves a nice blue point crab.

We were catching these crabs at a fairly fast pace. We took some of the mullet backbones from which we had cut chunk bait and pitched them in the water to draw more crabs. I had my little Orvis 100 spinning reel and rod with 6-pound-test line, so I took one of the backbones, hooked my white bucktail to it, and pitched it in. The backbone with the remnant meat was just what the crabs wanted, and I was bringing in two at a time! Did I mention that it was a 6-pound-test line?

A while later, as my bait once again began moving as if a crab were on it, I slowly and gently began pulling the resistance back toward the boat. This one seemed as if it had more than two crabs because it was a lot harder to move toward the boat. As it moved closer, the resistance increased. I reached for the net thinking I had gotten a huge haul of crabs. Slowly I lifted my rod to bring them to the surface.

As I watched, a dark shadowy area was rising toward the surface. At about the same time I realized that this was a jewfish, he swirled on the surface, throwing gallons of water everywhere, and headed away from us like a miniature freight train. He had swallowed the backbone and my bucktail as well.

Know that first and foremost, my dad was a meat fisherman. Put food on the table! Any of you who have read any of my features know of his obsession with jewfish. So, after him we went! Only, he wasn't going anywhere. He had run off about 50 yards and stopped.

We idled the boat over until we were right over him. The water was about 12 feet deep, but in the dark, tannic water, we could not see him. As we sat on top of him, he would occasionally move 2 or 3 feet in one direction or another. I kept the pressure on him, trying to lift him off the bottom, but he simply would not budge. Did I mention that I had a 6-pound-test line?

For over an hour we tried anything and everything with the fish with no success. On one occasion we took one of the boat paddles and poked it around him to get him to move. He would move only when he saw fit, and only where he wanted to move.

The definition of fishing includes patience, but after about two hours of attempting to budge this fish, my father had apparently run out of that particular commodity. I guess he figured that if the line had not broken by now, he might be able to apply a little more pressure.

At any rate, he took the line in his hand just where it entered the water, and began to lift. Low and behold, the fish began to rise! For just a moment we could see the entire fish about 4 feet under the water. And for a fleeting few, heart-pounding seconds I think we both thought that we might catch this fish. Did I mention that I had a 6-pound-test line?

The sound of taught monofilament line snapping could be heard all over the bay. The fish had seen the boat, and with one quick swirl he broke off and swam away.

The next 30 minutes was a school of sorts, taught by my father about the need to be prepared for something like this in the future. After all, had we hooked that fish on his outfit with 20-pound-test line, it would be in the cooler right now. We had just let 50 pounds of great eating jewfish steaks swim away, and that was hard for him to take.

I guess I didn't learn my lesson, because I still fish with 6-pound-test line when the urge arises; but, whenever I do, I am reminded of that day when I failed to expect the unexpected.

A Favorite Snook Hole

High school afternoons filled with fish...

Fishing rod in hand, I was walking the bank of Snapper Creek canal heading out to Biscayne Bay from Old Cutler Road. Every afternoon after school, I would head there with my spinning outfit and a few white bucktail jigs. I was looking for snook, and there were plenty of them there to be caught there.

Snapper Creek is one of the many canals that were dug in the past to help drain water from swampy land in South Florida. Today, it has a saltwater intrusion dam, and even after almost 50 years, it is a wild mangrove lined canal for its last mile into the bay.

I walked the north bank, which I believe is inaccessible now due to trespassing laws. As I walked, I made casts into the canal. I made them as parallel to the bank as I could in all the open spaces between the many Australian pines that lined the north bank. Every hundred feet or so, a small drainage ditch was cut into the berm on which I was walking. Those cuts usually held at least one small snook, and I approached each cut very cautiously.

Snook were everywhere at that time. The canal was full of them. On this trip, I caught no fewer than ten on the trek from the bridge to the bay. I caught that many or more on the way back as the sun began to set in the west.

I also caught as many jack crevalle as I wanted to catch – probably 30 or more both on the way out and on the way back. It was a bank angler's dream.

The snook were mostly short of the then 18-inch minimum length. I often thought that they might be one of the five species of snook that never gets bigger than 18 inches. I thought that way until we fished at the end of the canal on the point one day.

At the point where the canal enters Biscayne Bay, the mullet schools were thick early in the morning and late in the day. Small tarpon and some very large snook would be busting these schools in a feeding frenzy. All I had to do was get that Zara Spook I carried in a small box in my back pocket out there into the midst of them.

On this trip, I tied on the spook and waited for the mullet to start scattering. I was standing right on the point of land, looking south toward Gables-by-the-Sea, when a huge snook erupted in the middle of a big school of mullet. I cast beyond the school and began "walking the dog" back toward me.

WHOOSH! That snook erupted on my lure and took off like a freight train. He ran a lot of 10-pound-test line off my reel before he turned and started running sideways. Luckily, there were few mangroves for him to reach at the point.

For the next 15 minutes, it was that fish and me. I got him close, and he ran more line out. I fought him back, and he ran again. Curiously – and I never could figure out why – he never jumped.

After that long fight, I waded out about knee deep to meet this monster in the water. I got him turned over on his side and slid him toward me. I had no net or gaff, so I lipped him – even before lipping a fish was ever popular.

My guess then was that he weighed 25 to 30 pounds. His tail touched the ground when I held him, and his head was as high as my shoulders.

With no fanfare other than a pounding heart, no camera, and no witnesses, I released this big guy. I fished for a while longer at the point and caught a few jacks. As I began the walk back in the now dark evening, I wondered if he would make it. After all, it was a long fight on a hot day.

When I reached the first ditch, I heard that wonderful sound of a monster snook busting up a school of mullet back behind me. I looked back at the point and saw the splash, and I knew he was back at it, feeding once again.

That was many, many years ago. But, I have sources who tell me that the fishing is as good there now as it ever has been. Snook are there, and they can be caught. I'll suffer a few negative emails for this article – I'm giving away someone's "secret" fishing spot. But, believe me – it was a favorite for more people than me long before these folks ever came along!

Does Cabin Fever Ever Strike You?

After a cold winter, it's hard to sit at home and not fish…

On a day when most other fishermen would stay in bed, we decided to make a go of it and attempt to fish. The temperature was well below freezing and was forecast to stay that way for most of the day. A 20-knot wind only added to the pain we experienced running at half throttle.

Cabin fever. Everybody gets it eventually, and we all succumb to it at some point. It's a debilitating condition; it makes us do things that any sane person would avoid. There is no known medicinal remedy. Therapy is the only solution. That therapy would have you venture into the elements seeking a cure.

Note that the weather elements may or may not cause a cure. If it turns out to be balmy and nice, the fever only worsens when you get home. If the weather is cold, windy, and not fit for man or beast, as it was this day, the fever is abated, even if only for another few weeks.

I would guess the chill factor on my boat on this morning was well below zero. We were wrapped in many coats and sweaters;1970Seacraft

 I was reminded of Ralphie's young brother being dressed for school in that great seasonal movie, *A Christmas Story* – we "looked like a tick about to pop."

Fishing in this weather is at once good and bad. I suspect we were the only anglers that bought bait from the tackle shop. My regular shop was closed, as were three others we passed. We bought some live shrimp and mud minnows. Fiddlers have been nonexistent in tackle shops for over a week now. I have never figured out whether

115

the cold weather makes the fiddlers or the fiddler catchers disappear. My money would be on the latter based how cold I was!

The tide was high in the morning when we launched – a perfect morning tide. We ran to some small creek openings as the water began to fall and run off the surrounding grass and mud flats. If there were any redfish to be had, they should be coming off those flats.

Live shrimp and mud minnows are kept alive in my live well. It's a recirculating live well, constantly pumping fresh seawater through the tank, a numbing, 47-degree seawater. Losing your bait becomes a very unpleasant experience on a day like today. When I look at a tired mud minnow on my hook in the summertime, I am apt to replace him with a fresh, lively one. But, today, he stays on the hook for as long as I can manage to keep him. Somehow the tired bait looked just fine on days like this.

I often wonder what the fish do when they get lockjaw on these cold, high-pressure days. I know they don't bite. And although I can usually entice a few as the sun gets overhead, it still makes me wonder what is going on in their world. Perhaps it's because no self-respecting mud minnow or shrimp would be seen out on a day like this, and my bait is an obvious "out of place" picture to them.

Whatever the reason, we caught no fish. I let the mud minnows go at the dock and kept the majority of what was six-dozen live shrimp, which I boiled and had for dinner later that evening.

The bad news was we caught no fish. The good news was we caught no fish. The reason for the good news is threefold. First, we did not have to clean fish. Second, I had some really good boiled shrimp that night. Third, and probably most important, my cabin fever has abated.

I read the long-range forecast this morning. Saturday's outlook is for 20 to 25-knot winds and temperatures in the 20s again. Suddenly, a crackling fire, hot cup of coffee, a newspaper and the morning array of fishing shows on ESPN looked nice!

Stuck by a Saltwater Catfish

In all my years, I can truthfully say there is no other fishing pain like this one…

One of the worst pains in the world comes from being stuck by one of the spines of a saltwater catfish.

I'm sitting here typing with nine fingers. The 10th, my left thumb, is so swollen and sore that I can't use it. That's because a little over 24-hours ago I did what I never do with a saltwater catfish. I let my guard down. I let my guard down on a 5-inch long saltwater catfish, and he flopped one time and got me! Over my career, I have caught an uncountable number of these aggravating little fish, but as I search my files, I can only find one article I ever wrote about them. Well, here is No. 2!

We were on the inside of the inlet at Matanzas, just south of St. Augustine, Florida, when it happened. The beautiful sunrise and morning light on the old Spanish fort made the morning something really special. I was with my son and grandson, and we were planning on a banner day.

Matanzas Inlet is a small, narrow inlet protected by the shallow sandbars that cover its mouth. An ever-changing channel of sorts allows those anglers with some local, recent knowledge to exit to the ocean on a decent day. If the wind is up, however, as it was this morning, the breakers prevent anyone from even attempting to go out, and they default farther north to the deeper St. Augustine Inlet. Matanzas is not an inlet that is maintained with a U.S. Army Corps of Engineers dredged channel or markers. You take your chances, and sometimes people make the mistake of trying to save some fuel only to become involved in a swamped, overturned boat.

Fishing here was great (emphasis on "was"). Over the past week, friends of my son had been "tearing up" the redfish and mangrove snapper in the area. This area is home to mangrove trees that are as far north in Florida as any I know about. It's about 15 miles south of St. Augustine at the south end of what is now the Matanzas River. In the 1940s the Intracoastal Waterway (ICW) was cut though the river north and south, and the resulting weakened tidal flow over the years allowed the ocean entrance to the old river to fill in with sand.

It is also about as far north as I have found inshore mangrove snapper on a regular basis. I catch some larger ones farther north but it's always offshore on an artificial reef, and usually only in the summertime. Somewhere around this inlet, the water in the winter starts staying too cold for some fish. But these snapper and redfish were here and were caught this past week. Please notice the word "were." Today would be a bust, and we caught nothing to speak of – a few very small snappers, one bluefish, several giant pinfish and one small catfish…

Do not get stuck by a catfish (emphasis on "do not"!). My dad always warned whoever was fishing with him to avoid even touching a saltwater catfish – and in Florida Bay where he usually fished, they caught a bunch of them on any given trip. He knew the pain, and sadly as I grew up fishing with him, I learned about the pain firsthand on several occasions. You do not want even to get grazed by one of the three spines of a saltwater catfish!

I've been stuck by a dorsal fin or two of other fish many times over the years. I even had the big, first spine of the dorsal fin of a 208-pound Goliath grouper (jewfish) go through the calf muscle in my leg. It was like jamming a small Phillips head screwdriver in my leg! But the pain from even that stick was nothing in comparison to a saltwater catfish.

The three spines of a saltwater catfish are all loaded with toxins. One website describes them as a complex toxin made up of a mix of "high-molecular weight proteins and low-molecular weight compounds." Whatever that means technically, I'm not sure, but it sure means pain physically.

OK, I let my guard down, and that little fish stuck me. His dorsal fin went in my thumb along the side of my thumbnail, and as fast as it went in, it came back out. These fins are not like a smooth, needle point of a hook. The sides look like a saw blade, and as the fin comes out of the puncture point, it rips flesh out with it. That only serves to allow the toxins to spread more quickly in the wound.

As I sat, literally with tears running down my face, the pain only intensified. With help from my son, I filled a small Ziploc bag with crushed ice and wrapped it on and around my thumb. To my dismay, the pain only worsened over the next hour. I was nauseous and light-headed and could find no position to get my thumb to stop throbbing. After asking me about going in for the past hour, my son finally called it a day and thankfully demanded we head home.

When I got home, I immediately began researching, and much to my amazement I found several things I could do to relieve the pain. What is more amazing is that what I did worked. "Do not use ice or cold on the wound," said the internet article. Imagine my surprise on this one. It turns out that cold only makes the toxins more powerful. So I had the answer as to why the ice not only did not help but seemed to make the pain even worse! "Use hot water," it said. I would never have thought to do this one. But water above 105 degrees Fahrenheit will break down the molecular structure of the toxins and stop the pain. I found this out for myself a bit later in the shower. As the hot water soaked in on my thumb, the pain subsided, and during my shower, it stopped hurting. I was amazed!

"I'm in my boat, and we have no hot water – what do I do?" That's a good question. Almost every late model outboard has a "pee stream," a water stream off the side of the engine block that acts as a visual indicator that the water pump is working to cool the engine. The water in that stream is hot enough to do the job! If you have an engine that has no stream, try pouring hot coffee or tea or soup that you may have in a thermos onboard.

This last option would be my last resort, but many commercial fishermen who get stuck quite often tell me they urinate or have their buddy urinate on the wound. They say it helps stop the pain. Whether it's the warmth of the liquid or something chemical – who knows? Is it safe? I don't know. Will it cause further problems like an infection? I don't know. I am told that urine is quite sterile and will cause no problem. Would I recommend it? No – I'm just reporting what I found!

The trick in all of this is simply this: Don't get stuck! Bring a fish gripper tool or pliers or anything that can safely grab the fish. If it looks like it's going to get messy, cut the hook off! I would much rather lose a hook than gain a saltwater catfish fin!

Fort Macon Albies

Catching false albacore from the shore with tackle that was way too light...

The air was crisp as we walked down the beach, crisp enough to more than hint at the coming of fall weather. Oh, for some good fall weather to turn on the fish on the North Carolina shore!

The sign on the beach indicated we were entering Fort Macon State Park on the tip of the Atlantic Beach barrier island protecting Morehead City and Beaufort. The Newport River enters here from the ocean, and the inlet forms a natural fish migration path. Flounder, trout, bluefish, stripers, virtually all of the coastal species will swim this cut during this time of year.

We had parked in the Coast Guard base parking lot just before the State Park and were making the trek down the beach to the jetties. All of our fishing party were Marines from Cherry Point, and the military parking sticker lets us into the Coast Guard base. We parked and walked the beach because the gate to the state park did not open until 8 a.m. and that's a good two hours later than we needed to get the early bite.

Carrying a bucket of finger mullet we had caught with our cast net on the bay side of the inlet, we made our way out on the large rock slabs that make up the jetties.

Some of the slabs are at such an angle that they can't be walked on easily, and that made the trip to the end even more difficult. Once on the end, we took up our places on the flattest rocks and began rigging our rods. As I looked down the beach, I could see the huge cloud of birds working the surf and moving in our direction. They were gulls, about 100 strong, and they were over a huge school of false albacore. The albacore were gorging themselves as they moved toward the jetties, following an equally huge school of bait fish.

They were about a half mile away and moving in by the time we were ready for them. I had an old, freshwater, top water bait, a Creek Chub Darter as I remember, tied to 6 feet of wire leader on a 7-foot spinning outfit. No fish was going to get off on this trip! Our last two trips to the jetties found us with the same situation: a morning surf feed of Albies and us with small light tackle. We lost every bait in our tackle boxes to these 20 pounders as they moved through. This time would be different. We had spent the previous evening tying long wire leaders and spooling 20- and 30-pound test line on much larger gear. So here we were, ready for the onslaught!

As the school moved closer, our hearts raced. Everywhere in every direction, blue and white 20-pound bullets were leaping in the air. Baitfish were jumping everywhere! Birds were screaming and diving, and it appeared as if even the birds would be taken by one of the leaping, eating machines! And the closer they came, the louder the noise became.

We waited. We waited for the fish to get into casting range. We knew we would have only about 15 minutes of fishing because, at the end of that time, the school would have moved on, as they had the previous three days. And so we waited.

And then, when it seemed as if we were going to burst with anticipation, one of us made the first cast. Zing went the silver spoon across the top of the water. The plunking sound of the spoon entering the water reached us at the same time the sound of the screaming drag did. And for John, the fight was on. Zing went another cast, this one from Richard, and another drag screamed.

And then it was my turn. I cast my bucktail across the top of the water, and it never hit the surface. A blur of blue streaked out of the water from 5 feet away and grabbed the bucktail in midair! What a fight! My fish headed for parts unknown and ran almost half the line from my reel. A small piece of weed dangled on my line right at the point of water entry, moving up and down and in and out of the water with every head shake of my fish. That movement was all it took. In a split second another blur of blue came down on the dangling weed, mistaking it for something live. And immediately I realized we would be hard-pressed to keep up with these fish.

In what seemed like only a few seconds, 15 minutes had passed, and the school had moved on. Among the three of us, we had one fish. Mine got cut off by another fish, and John's pulled free from what we considered to be too much drag. But, oh what a thrill! We would make this trip several more mornings before the fish decided to migrate on, and we would lose most of our tackle. But for a week that year, we had a ball catching false albacore from the Fort Macon Jetties.

Grouper with No Holes

With no fishing tackle apparent, how in the world did these grouper get caught?

My dad was fishing with his brother-in-law, H.A. one day in the '60s at Flamingo. Pop was down for his annual one or two week stay in one of the cabins there at the end of the 40-mile road from Florida City. He stayed the entire time, while friends and relatives made their reservations with him to stay a day or two at a time. He would have the entire time scheduled out, and he fished every day.

They were fishing in Florida Bay south of Flamingo and had decided to do a little exploring to look for new places to fish. They ended up going through Man-of-War Channel and across Blue Bank through Iron Pipe Channel, one of the many, small, natural channels that cut through the bank. That put them in Rabbit Key Basin, an area 2 or 3 miles in diameter that was bordered on the west by Blue Bank and the east by the two Rabbit Keys.

A small channel led up to the two keys, partially natural, but I suspect mainly formed from the prop wash of many commercial fishermen during those days. Commercial fishing was permitted back then, but only by hook and line. Nets were not allowed. The channel ran directly up to the keys which, like so many other mangrove islands in Florida Bay, had comparatively deep water right up next to the mangroves. That deep water was formed from the tidal currents that swept past the island. Bernoulli's effect is at play on these islands, and the current is much stronger when it goes around the ends of the island – much like the wind in Chicago when it rips around the tall buildings. That swifter current has cut out the deep holes on the ends of the islands.

The channel going up to the islands allowed boats to get past the shallow water surrounding the islands and into the next basin. The water was and still is pristine. It is clear, clean and home to a variety of marine life. The basin averages about 10 feet deep with many white potholes scattered through the turtle grass bottom. These potholes are a foot or two deeper than the surrounding bottom, and they are easily seen from the surface because of their white color.

Pop and H.A. had eased into the channel headed to Rabbit Keys. Like all the local channels, small stakes marked the way. They had anchored on the edge of that channel to fish, and I believe to eat lunch when my father saw them. Spiny lobster (aka crawfish) antennae were sticking out from the edge of the grass along each side of the little channel. According to Pop, they were everywhere.

That was my first knowledge of any crawfish being in Florida Bay. We dove all over south Florida, in Biscayne Bay and out on the patch reefs for crawfish, but never thought about Florida Bay.

In the '60s diving was legal in Everglades National Park as long as you did not have a spear-gun. The water in some of the deeper cuts there was clear and beautiful, and many people dove there just to cool off on a hot day if nothing else.

Four of us high school buddies decided to try diving in the park one Saturday, given the story Pop had related to us. We were in his boat, so he made sure he called and talked to the park personnel about taking crawfish. It turned out to be legal, so he gave us his stamp of approval. Of course, I believe the thought of a few crawfish with his name on them helped with his decision.

We went to Rabbit Key basin, found a likely, white, pothole and anchored the boat. Once over the side, our eyes popped out. There were lobsters everywhere, and we quickly had our limit of 24 in the boat. We didn't bring any fishing tackle, so once we had our limit we came back in and headed home.

We could have gone through Biscayne Bay off Elliot Key to the patch reefs and gotten our limit and burned far less gas, but the patch reefs were much deeper than Rabbit Key Basin. This was easy diving.

We found what was, at the time, a loop hole in the crawfish regulations. Everyone was using this loop hole up and down the Florida Keys, and we were no exception. It seems the limit was 24 crawfish per boat, but nothing was in the rules regarding a possession limit. So, the next time we went, we took two boats. As soon as we got 24 crawfish in the boat, we ran that boat back in to the dock and put them in a big cooler. By the time we ran that boat back out, the other boat had 24 and they headed in to do the same thing. I think the most we ever got in one day was 120. That was five trips back to the dock and it was legal at the time. We were even approached by a park ranger at the dock. He congratulated us on our catch!

Of course the law soon changed and a possession limit of 24 was placed on the lobster. That stopped our two-boat-effort, but it didn't stop our diving. On one particular trip we were taking lobsters from the coral rock holes in the sides and bottom of a Rabbit Key Basin pothole. Spiny lobsters always backed into these holes with their antennae sticking out. Unlike their northern cousins in Maine, they have no claws. They defend themselves with those long, spiny antennae.

The trick to catching them was to get your gloved hand under their belly, then grab them and pull them out. Sometimes they would kick back farther into the hole and you would have to reach farther into the hole, feeling your way around.

What scared me when it first happened was the soft, slimy thing I felt on the roof of one hole. If I pushed on it, it would grunt. I rubbed my hand one direction, and it was fish-slimy smooth. The other direction had the feeling of scales. It was a fish! To be exact, it was a small red grouper.

After surfacing and getting more air I went back down and put my arm into that hole. I felt my way around until I found the head of the fish, and with one gloved finger in an eye socket and one inside his top lip, I grabbed and pulled a 3-pound grouper out of the hole and tossed it into the boat.

It tuned out that many of these holes had grouper hiding in them. They would position themselves flat against the roof of the hole, such that if you peered into the hole, you would not see them.

We were having a ball catching crawfish and grouper, right up until a park ranger boat came to where we were. That in itself was not unusual. We had been checked numerous times in the past. But this time, the young ranger, who was on his first week of the job in Everglades National Park, was particularly interested in the grouper. Having been transferred from Yellowstone, he was not familiar with saltwater fishing or diving. After counting and measuring our crawfish – they had to have a 3-inch carapace – he turned his attention to the grouper. We had maybe four or five of them in the ice chest.

He carefully inspected each grouper and then began looking around our boat.

"Where is all your fishing tackle?"

"We don't have any. We're diving."

"Well, where did these grouper come from?"

"We caught them by hand."

And at that point, he began a more in-depth search of every nook and cranny of the boat. When we asked what he was searching for he told us he was looking for a spear gun. When he found none, he accused us of pitching the spear gun overboard when he approached.

Of course we had no spear gun. We took each grouper and asked him to look for a hole that would have been made by a spear. And, of course, he found none. We explained how we caught them, even showed him the grip we used to pull the fish out of the hole.

I'm not sure he was satisfied, but he had to leave us alone because we had done nothing wrong. As we talked and he calmed down, Paul asked if he could go over the side and show him what we did.

Paul went down and in just a few minutes surfaced hollering that he found another grouper. He gulped some air, went back down and after a minute or so came back to the surface with another grouper firmly in his grip. The ranger's eyes almost popped out of his head, and he broke into a big smile.

Paul flipped the fish over the gunnel and said to the ranger, "See if you can find a hole in that one!"

The park is closed to diving these days. Crawfish are protected inside the park, and Rabbit Key Basin has been declared a nursery for the spiny lobster. In other parts of Florida, the limit is now 6 per person with a one-day possession limit. It's a considerable change from when we dove and caught so many.

Oh, by the way, there is no specification in the spiny lobster regulations regarding any holes or lack of holes in any fish that may be on board...

Brain Coral Grouper

In high school, we often ended up diving on the patch reefs off Elliot Key in South Florida. It's amazing what teenagers can do…

It's Sunday afternoon, and the four of us are diving out of my father's boat. The rule was if I went to church I could take out the boat Sunday afternoon. Bribery? Probably. Nevertheless, we took advantage of the opportunity.

We seldom used any scuba gear. Even though there was no requirement for certification at the time. All we had to do to rent a couple of tanks, regulators and weight belts was pay the man the money and leave a driver's license with him for security. We rented them during the lobster season to facilitate a faster catch, or when the water where we wanted to dive was deeper than we could comfortably free dive.

Today the water was about 15 feet deep, and we were anchored over a huge brain coral that rose up off the bottom about 8 feet. It was probably 8 feet in diameter, and as we discovered it had a big hole under it on the bottom which allowed us to see light coming from the other side. It was surrounded by big sea fans and smaller coral formations, and lots of fish.

We all had our Hawaiian slings, an underwater slingshot of sorts that shot a spear through a small tube using surgical tubing. We also had one double-rubber Arbalete spear gun which we took turns using. It was much more accurate and powerful than our slings.

Diving down on the brain coral, we were looking for any what we considered to be edible fish: snapper, grouper, hogfish, it didn't matter as long as it was great to eat.

One gulp of air and a kick or two from our fins got us to the bottom, and we began inspecting that brain coral. Without weight belts, it was hard to stay on the bottom without bobbing back toward the surface. So we held on to the edges of the brain coral and looked underneath it.

As I peered under and saw the light coming from the other side, something moved across under the coral and blocked the light. An eerie feeling came over me as I wondered what kind of monster might lurk under that coral.

As soon as we had all seen the "monster" block the light, we decided to take the Arbalete down and try to shoot it. So one of us went down, held the edge of the coral and when the darkness came, fired a spear into the unknown. By that time we were out of air, so we dropped the spear gun and headed back to the surface. Another gulp of air sent us back down to retrieve the gun, the spear and whatever it was on the end of the spear. The spear had a line attached to its aft portion, and the gun was designed to float. Any fish could be handled by simply retrieving the gun and pulling the line and spear back to you.

As it turned out it was a fish, a nice grouper. We thought we had struck gold!

After we repeated this feat several times, Don came up shouting he had hit a grouper, but that something had taken hold of it. He played tug-o-war with whatever it was until he had the grouper he had speared half way out from under the coral.

What he saw then was a moray eel which had the other half of the grouper in its teeth. And after one more tug, the spear came out, and the moray won the battle for the fish.

Don swam toward the boat in a panic. It seems this 6-foot long moray eel had appeared on the scene without us seeing him. We were not sure whether the eel was a resident under that coral or whether the fish blood from several grouper had attracted him. It didn't matter because he was there and he was aggressive. Usually reclusive and avoiding any human interaction, this moray was in and out and around the hole and would come completely out to swim toward a diver if the diver got close enough.

I'm not afraid of much under the water. Don was afraid of even less. We swam with huge barracudas watching us. We swam with sharks that were cruising the area. It was only if one of them began looking aggressive that would cause us to exit the water. But a moray? Man, they are one mean looking creature with a full set of razor-sharp teeth.

We sat in the boat and debated about what to do. There were many more grouper down there, but the moray would not let us get near them.

We devised a plan, flipped a coin to see who would be executing the plan, and then went back into the water. As long as we floated on the surface, the moray stayed under the coral, occasionally poking his head out to watch us.

Don, the winner – or maybe I should say loser – on the coin toss was assigned the task of shooting the moray with the Arbalete. The plan was to shoot it and let go of the gun. We had tied extra line to the spear so that the gun would float all the way to the surface.

So, as two of us watched while floating on the surface, Don dove with the spear gun. Fortunately, the shot he took was a good one, and the spear penetrated the eel.

At that point, there was a circus playing out on the stern of our boat as we all fought to get out of the water. Once we were all in the boat we looked and saw the spear gun floating close to the boat. We retrieved the gun and slowly began pulling the spear back to the boat.

Impaled on the end of the spear and wound up into a big, slithering ball was our monster. It was mad and it was striking out at anything close to it, almost like a snake. I don't know how it could see while out of the water, but it could at least make out shapes that were close by.

Now we needed to somehow dispatch this monster so we could get on with our grouper-fest. The problem was that we had no knife. We had no way to get this eel off our spear, and without the Arbalete we would not get another grouper.

We were on my dad's boat, a 1957 Squall King, and he always had a spare anchor. We located the anchor and as we held the eel and spear on the gunnel of the boat, we began using the anchor as a hammer. We pretty much beat the head off that eel, and at the same time took several chunks of gelcoat off the gunnel – something I would pay dearly for a few days later… As the grip it had on the spear loosened, we noticed a bulge in the middle portion of moray. It was the grouper he stole!

With no knife to cut the fish out, we began squeezing the eel from the bottom and moving the fish toward what was left of the head. Like a tube of toothpaste, the grouper came up out of the belly of our monster. Amazingly, the grouper was still moving its gills.

We speared another few out from under that brain coral before heading home. We did eat the "eaten" grouper, and all the rest as well, but I remember a discussion around what sort of digestive poison the eel may have imparted to that grouper. Not to worry, that was about 55 years ago, and Don and I are still kicking!

The Legend of
Captain Walter Mann

A fisherman's fisherman if there ever was one…

As a kid back in the 50s and 60s I fished with my dad. Any time the boat went into the water, I was in it with him. There were only a few occasions as I grew up that I did not fish when he fished. One of the great parts of fishing back then for me was to listen to the grown-ups. While I was always fishing when my dad fished, he usually took along a friend or co-worker, which meant there were almost always three of us in the boat.

The boat had a covered bow and windshield, and the usable fishing area was confined to the back of the boat. I, on the other hand, was usually confined to the bow of the boat. I was the anchorman. Drop the anchor - pull the anchor - sit on the bow and hold on while we were running. I thought very little about it back then - hey, I was fishing with my dad!

I would listen to the two men talk about fishing all the way to the boat ramp, a trip that took about 90 minutes including stops for bait and ice. There were tales of fish caught the previous trip; there were descriptions of the battle with a big jewfish (Goliath grouper) that broke off on the last trip; and, there were discussions about where we would fish that day. All of this fascinated me from the back seat of the car. I spoke very little but listened a whole lot with my chin resting on the top of the front seat back.

I remember several discussions about some of the guides where we usually fished. Flamingo, in the Everglades National Park, was home base for several very good guides back then. It still is today, but somehow today's guides just don't measure up to the legends I remember back then.

The talk would center on where they saw a particular guide the last trip, whether he was catching fish, and always, always about how they wished they could go with one of them just one time.

The guide that garnered the most talk was Captain Walter Mann. I can remember seeing him in his boat. As I remember it, his boat was an inboard cuddy of some type, around 24 feet in length with a wide beam. It appeared to be all wood with a windshield and partial top coming back toward the stern. Underway it probably could do 18 to 20 knots at top speed. But my memory is of the boat trudging along

at about 10 to 12 knots, headed to a fishing spot that Captain Mann had chosen. My dad would always comment on how he took a long time to get where he was going, but he always caught fish. He never seemed to be in a hurry. In the '60s it was not uncommon to fish all day out of Flamingo and never see another boat. Today, of course, you sometimes have to take turns and get in line to fish a particular flat. On those days where we saw no one else, it was always a good sign to see Captain Mann. I mean, if he is fishing the same area that we are fishing, then we must be where the fish are, right? That was our assumption, and it was an accurate one.

Captain Mann, as the legend was told to me, spent a lot of time fishing Flamingo. I can remember my father telling me that Captain Mann fished every day for two full years before he took a paying charter out at Flamingo. During that time, he kept a log of water, weather, tide, location, and catch. There was lots of talk about wishing that we could get that log book in our hands!

The story as given to me about the log is as accurate in my mind as my dad's stories about it. I often wondered just how much of the story was true and how much of it was embellished simply by Captain Mann's presence. I felt like I just wanted to go touch him at the dock if he would let me - he was that much of a "famous" person to me.

When I fish, I watch the tide. I have some locations I only fish on an outgoing tide, and some only at the bottom of the outgoing tide. I have places I fish on a high slack tide. And at all of the locations I fish, the bite lasts for about an hour, and it's over. I, along with most other anglers, have learned that the tide plays a big role in just when the fish will be in a particular location, and when they will feed. When I look back at the days of Captain Mann, I can see he was years ahead of his time. That log book could tell him that on a July day with an outgoing tide in the morning he could find seatrout on the back side of a particular grass flat. Or, he could drop a live shrimp along a particular channel edge at dead high tide and catch big mangrove snapper. He was playing the tides before people knew how to play the tides!

My dad finally splurged one year and, along with my uncle and myself, booked a trip with Captain Mann. We went from Flamingo all the way up toward Rogers River along the Southwest Florida coast. In Captain Mann's boat that was a long trip. But we went in my dad's Squall King, and the trip took much less time. We could hire him to go in his boat or ours; it was obviously cheaper to take him in ours.

Captain Mann tied up to a mangrove branch and, as my dad complained, "sat and wasted time." My dad grabbed a rod while Captain Mann - as I said, he was never one to get in a hurry - told him to relax and eat a sandwich. The fish would not bite for another 30 minutes.

Well, by Ned, my dad paid to fish, and he was going to fish. As he fished for the next 30 minutes, he never got so much as a nibble. And then the tide changed.

Captain Mann, with the ever present stogie in his mouth, took a rod, cast it over toward another mangrove branch, and handed it to my dad. Wham! A redfish grabbed the bait before it ever got to the bottom. And for the next hour, we - mostly they - caught one red after another, with trout and mangrove snapper mixed in.

To say that my dad was amazed was an understatement! I was just in awe of this man that I simply wanted to touch!

We went back to that same mangrove branch to fish - just my dad and me - on several occasions. Only a few times did we catch fish, and we never put one and one together to come up with the tide. The times we caught fish were the times that the tide was right. Old Captain Mann didn't mind us fishing where he fished. He knew from his log book that the fish would not be there except for a short window of opportunity - the right tide.

One of Captain Mann's favorite fish, if not his very favorite, was the jewfish. He held the record at Flamingo for many years. I think that one of the reasons we gravitated toward Captain Mann was that the jewfish was also my dad's favorite. Our problem was that we had a hard time catching a big one. Oh, how we wanted to go through that log book and look for jewfish holes!!

I had Captain Mann on my mind this past month - don't know why just sitting and reminiscing about the great fishing of my youth. I was wondering what happened to him and what happened to his log book. If he were still alive, he would have to be in his 90s or older.

That same day, an email came to me from a young lady in South Florida. I have mentioned Captain Mann in some of my other articles, and it seems she had been searching for information about Captain Walter Mann. Young Jamie was writing me to find out about her grandfather!

We exchanged a few emails and she sent the picture you see here of her grandfather in his boat. She was only two years old when he died, and she was trying to gather as much information about him as she could. Even though she does not remember him, he is as much or more of a legend in her mind as he is in mine.

Oh, the logbook! What about Captain Mann's logbook? Was it real? Did it exist?

It turns out that it is in fact real. As I write this Jamie is attempting to gain access to it. It's in a safety deposit box that belongs to a relative.

The pages are yellowed and brittle, and it appears that it may fall apart if it is handled too much; but, yes it does exist and it does contain all of his fishing haunts and holes.

I have a zillion questions going through my mind right now. All of them are about the who, what, where, when and why of that book. I feel like Indiana Jones finally finding the Holy Grail and not being able to touch it!

Jamie has offered to send any pictures she comes across and is going to try and photograph the logbook for me. When she does that, I will be right back with you here to tell you about it! Oh, and that second picture? That's my dad and me with the first "big" jewfish we caught. It's hanging on the same winch at the same dock where Captain Mann hung all of his fish for pictures. And the Squall King is tied at the dock behind us.

Until Jamie finds more pictures, I can just sit back and remember a great old fisherman, cigar and all, who took his time, never got in a hurry, and always "magically" caught fish!

The Snook at Slagle's Ditch

I firmly believe I was the luckiest man alive when I married my childhood sweetheart...

It was 1962, and I was in high school. I fished almost every Saturday with my dad and usually one of his friends from work. This particular Saturday that friend was his boss, Mr. Carter. After driving from his home in Hollywood, Florida, he arrived at our house about 4 a.m., the usual time we left to fish.

The drive to Flamingo was about two hours if you included the stops for bait and ice. That put us in the water just after daybreak. It also put us at the boat ramp at the worst possible time for mosquitoes and sand gnats.

But we had the launching routine down to almost a science and the bugs were gone by the time we got up on a plane in the channel. The cool, damp air of an early morning summer day blew the bugs out as I helped run them up from the back of the boat out from under the gunnels.

Good old Mr. Carter. He was older than my dad and was the most kind, gentle, soft-spoken person I believe I had ever met. He never complained about anything. He was also almost legally blind.

My dad, on the other hand, was deaf in one ear and could hardly hear out of the other. He wore a hearing aid that hung from his undershirt – my dad always wore an undershirt – with a very visible wire that connected the amplifier to his ear piece. He was almost deaf.

The story, as they told it about one trip they made, centered on the heavy fog. They left the dock in a fog so thick they could barely see their hands in front of them let alone the markers. My dad was idling the boat along at the side console toward the aft end of the boat. Mr. Carter was standing on the casting deck at the bow looking for the channel markers ahead of them.

Here was a blind man looking for markers, directing in a soft voice a man who could not hear, to tell him which way to turn the boat. The vision of that encounter brings tears to my eyes because I laugh so hard. They never said how they finally got out the channel. Suffice it to say they did.

On this morning there was no fog as we headed out. The weather was calm, and it was going to prove to be a very hot day on the water. As we headed west from Flamingo, the first place we stopped was Slagle's Ditch, a small dredged canal that ran north into the interior of the swamp.

This canal, along with several others, was dug in the early 1900s by the old Flagler Land Company in a futile effort to "drain the swamp," as Henry Flagler put it.

As we were idling toward the mouth of the ditch, we could see fish striking sometimes several at a time right in the mouth. These were not small fish, no, they were snook!

Bait and fishing lure preferences change from time to time with fishermen. It has been said that fishing lures are designed to catch fishermen more than they are to catch fish. I agree! The lure of preference on this trip was a solid red, butterbean, bucktail jig. We tied all our jigs, and these were a deep red color. I think someone stumbled on a color that caught fish on a particular day and the word spread.

We had the usual 12 dozen live shrimp in our live-bait garbage can. Built-in live wells were unheard of back then. If you fished with live bait, you used a 20-gallon plastic garbage can with an aerator that clipped to the boat's battery. The garbage can had a wooden lid that had a hinged cover, and the aerator ran all day. We never fished without 12 dozen live shrimp.

We always carried a wooden dowel pole on the boat. It was 2 inches in diameter and almost as long as the boat. We kept it tied to the boat gunnel as we ran. It was used as an anchor of sorts. Instead of having to drop the anchor at every stop, we could use this pole if the water was shallow and had a soft bottom.

We quietly drifted toward the mouth with me on the bow holding that pole. I used it to push the boat along, many years before poling became popular. When my dad gave me the signal, I pushed the pole into the soft bottom and tied the bow line to it.

It was now time to fish, and the snook were striking everywhere. What followed was almost like a circus act of clowns.

We could hook a snook on almost every cast. We would hook the jig to a live shrimp through the head and cast. Lift three times and reel. Lift three times and reel. Wham! That's literally how it went.

We had two snook on most of the time and three of them hooked up several times. These were hard-running, jumping, fighting fish and my dad tried to net every one of them. The problems began because he was netting with one hand while fighting a fish with the other.

More than once he netted two fish at a time because they had crossed our lines so badly. But, when all three of us got tangled with three fish, the net went away. Twice he grabbed the three tangled lines together and lifted three fish into the boat.

Have you noticed you haven't read the word "release?" We had snook flopping all over the deck of the boat. We had to watch our step to make sure we didn't step on one.

I think it was because my dad feared the wide-open bite would end that he just brought the fish in and kept fishing. We had an ice chest with fresh ice and no fish in it!

At some point, the circus ended, and the striking fish left us. Maybe we caught all of them; I don't know. But the bite was over. As we caught our breath and looked at all the snook in the boat, my dad told me to come off the bow and help him.

One by one he picked the fish up and placed them on the measuring lines he had etched into the boat, tail on one end and nose of the fish on the other. There were two notches etched into the fiberglass floor; one was 12 inches for seatrout and the other 18 inches for snook.

Amazingly, if the snook was less than 18 inches, the legal minimum length, he tossed it back in the water. I say amazingly because when he had finished measuring all the fish and releasing the short ones, we had 22 snook in our cooler – the bag limit was two per person. I'm thinking to myself that if you're going to break the law on the bag limit, why not the length limit as well? He had a few quirky reasoning moments in his life!

We could not get the lid closed on the ice chest with all those snook inside, so my dad pulled gray tarp from under the bow of the boat. He folded it so it could drape over the ice chest, and then he tied the anchor rope around it. All the time he was doing this he was scanning the horizon for another boat. This was Everglades National Park, and there is no telling what the consequences of being caught would be.

We immediately headed back in to the dock. Mr. Carter quietly asked if we were going to fish some more. My dad either ignored him or didn't hear him.

It was probably the fastest boat retrieval exercise we had ever been through. With the boat on the trailer, we headed out of the park and back home. The entire 75-mile trip made my dad look like a nervous wreck as he watched for a nonexistent, official car following us.

It was only after we backed the boat into our driveway that he relaxed. I looked at my watch. It was 10:45 a.m. The entire trip was about six hours. Excluding the driving there and back, the fishing time was about two hours.

My dad was usually honest to a fault. He never went over the speed limit, to the point he could become a traffic hazard. He never cheated on his taxes. To my knowledge he never stole anything. Maybe he borrowed a couple of screwdrivers and pliers from the phone company where he worked, but he always explained that they were going to be thrown away. That's about it. He was an honest man!

But when it came to fishing, he lost his composure on this trip. He never did anything like that again. I think perhaps his conscience got to him. In later years he followed every fishing rule to the letter.

We caught a lot of snook over the years, and many of those came from Slagle's Ditch. We kept two per person until the limits changed and then we kept only one. He was honest about his fishing.

The Net Rack

No longer visible above the water line, these old pilings provided us with many fish over the years.

When we began fishing together at Flamingo in Everglades National Park in the '50s, my father introduced me to some history from his youth when we headed for the net rack. Only about 3 miles from the boat ramp, this set of telephone pole pilings sat in the water just off the entrance channel to Snake Bight. According to him, the commercial fishermen used this rack to dry their nets.

Seine nets were not only legal but were often the preferred method for the commercial boys to catch fish. Drying their nets after a catch meant stretching them out on a frame and letting the sun do its work. If it rained on them, all the better for the life of the net because the rain removed the saltwater.

When we fished around the net rack, there were 16 telephone pole-sized pilings making a square of four rows with four pilings each. For a few years, the remnant of a deck that used to be sitting on the poles was present. But over the years, the rack became, except for a few cross-members, just the 16 pilings.

The water surrounding the net rack was relatively shallow. Sitting on the corner of the channel into Snake Bight where "Tin Can Ally" heads east, it was only about a half mile or so from Joe Kemp Key. Tin Can Alley got its name, according to my dad, from the tin cans that marked the channel. Locals had driven small stakes into the mud bottom, and because they were hard to see sometimes, they put an empty beer or soda can on top.

Both the Alley and the Snake Bight channel could be 5 or 6 feet deep at high tide. But the flats would be shallow and sometimes out of the water at low tide. Surprisingly, the water right under and adjacent to the net rack was 18 to 20 feet deep. Stories from some of the old-timers at the dock told of a fish house that sat on the pilings. The deeper water had been dredged to accommodate a larger vessel that would haul the fish catch to Key West. I'm not sure how accurate the stories were, but it makes sense to me.

We always fished the net rack at slack tide. It didn't matter whether it was high or low, we just needed still water. You see, we were after jewfish, and two things were certain: First, that one or more jewfish would be under the rack; and second, that they would feed on the slack tide. In most cases, we were right on both counts!

Over the years we caught more jewfish than I can remember under the net rack. Some were as small as 20 pounds; others were as large as 60 pounds. If we had been fishing the Cape Sable area or down south into Florida Bay, we would make the short detour to the net rack if we knew the tide would be slack. We seldom went directly there and fished all day, although we did fish the immediate area for snook, tarpon, and tripletail

The trip I remember most was one that included my dad, me and my good friend Don Carmichael. We had pulled up and tied off on the net rack and dropped a live bait on a handline right down into the pilings. We sat and baked waiting for a bite.

When the rope began twitching and moving off, my dad set the hook with his arms, and the fight was on. Only the fish did not want to come straight to the boat. It wound itself around several of the barnacle-encrusted pilings, making a cutoff very possible.

Not wanting to lose this fish, my father hopped up onto the net rack with the rope. He began trying to unwind the tangle from pole to pole. But the rope was hung. We could see the tail of the jewfish. It was apparently pinned to a pole in a head down position.

With little progress, Don decided to help out. Don stripped to his shorts and went into the water. So now we have my dad on the pilings and Don in the water. Don would follow the rope down, then come back up and tell my dad which direction it was wrapped. I was in the boat ready with the gaff. After what seemed like an eternity, the rope came clear, the fish surfaced, and we gaffed it into the boat. Success!

Immediately, my dad rebaited and put the rope down into the pilings again. He surmised that if one fish was in the pilings, there might be more. And it didn't take long for the rope to begin playing out.

As we set the hook and began pulling the rope in, the fish just seemed to come toward the surface with little fight. Remember now that Don has just been in that water diving around the pilings.

We pulled, and the fish rose. Only this was no ordinary fish. It was a shark that was almost as long as our 17-foot boat! He had not realized he was hooked, I think, because he didn't seem bothered by everything that was going on.

My dad yelled, "Cut the rope! Cut the rope! Cut the rope!" Being the ever obedient son, I grabbed the bait knife and cut the rope. The shark just slowly sank back down into the water.

I looked over at Don as he sat watching. He said nothing, but his eyes were as big as silver dollars! There is no telling how much damage that huge shark could have caused. There is also no telling what that shark would have done to Don!

Don and I fished many times over the years, and we still stay in touch and fish occasionally. But, nothing we have done can compare to this one trip to the net rack at Flamingo.

Secret Fishing Spots

Some anglers call them honey holes…

Secret fishing spots, some anglers call them honey holes, often get passed from father to son through generations. Of course, the reality is that our secret spots probably aren't as secret as we think they are. We may only get to them every few weeks while other anglers visit them in between without our knowledge.

I had some LORAN numbers at one time for locations off South Florida that I thought no one else knew. I fished the area on occasion, taking care not to let anyone mark my spot.

I even went so far as to pick up and move if a boat headed in my direction. Maybe you have done the same thing. Maybe you have done as I have when I saw a drifting or anchored boat with a hooked fish. I moved as close as I dared and then hit "mark" on my GPS. I would come back later and investigate the area looking for structure and live bottom.

There are, however, some fishing spots that never required a LORAN or GPS. Some were (and still are) back in Whitewater Bay in Everglades National Park. At least some of them are in small creeks that I may never again be able to fish.

I remember one in particular that saved many a trip on a bad day. When the winds howled, and there was no way to fish "out front" of Flamingo or in the Gulf of Mexico, this is one place we could count on to catch fish. I'll tell you exactly where it is because as of the last rule changes in the park, it is officially now a no-entry area.

My first experience with this particular fishing hole came on a day when we had caught nothing and had reverted to some exploring.

We were half-way across Lake Ingraham inside Cape Sable very close to the only island in the lake. Ingraham is a saltwater tidal bay

147

completely enclosed with an entry canal on each end. It's easy to find on any map.

East Cape Canal enters the lake on the south side, and Middle Cape Canal enters on the west side. The incoming and outgoing tides are brutally swift, and they bring sediment into the lake while they wash the canal banks away. Over the years these two canals have more than tripled in width from their original dredging. The current is strong and fast, to say the least.

Both of these canals were dug in the 1920s to help in the foolish and wasted effort by the Flagler Land Co.to drain the everglades. The tidal flow into and out of the lake has kept both canals deep and navigable over the years, although the lake itself seldom exceeds 4 feet deep.

A single channel, marked with small sticks, makes its way across the lake from end to end. On a good day with clear water, you simply follow the prop path that has been made by boats running the channel.

On the west end of the lake, the remnants of a coquina and concrete wall marked the entrance to Middle Cape Canal at one time. My father used to tell me stories about a man he called "Old man Brown," who, with his family, lived in a house there on the bank of Middle Cape canal. He caught shrimp for a living and, according to my dad, a small seaplane used to land in the lake and pick up the shrimp he had to sell.

If you have never been in this area in the summertime, having me tell you about how bad the mosquitoes are is fruitless. I can't imagine in my wildest dreams living with them. The southwest tip of Florida gets my vote for the most populated place in the world for saltwater mosquitoes. I guess it was another time and it took a different breed of individuals to live there.

The wall is gone now, washed away by the swift tidal currents that flood and drain the lake every six hours or so - a small piece of history that will go untold, except for those of us who remember.

Half way across the lake heading west, an island sits to the north of the channel. Many of my fishing hours have been spent drifting the grass to the south of the channel for redfish. Many of my hours were also spent trying to get the boat up on a plane and in the channel after we had fished all the way to low tide.

My dad told me stories about renting a small skiff at Slagle's Ditch in the '30s and running all the way to the lake with a 5-horsepower air-cooled Mercury. Some of those trips meant paddling back because of motor trouble. I was always enthralled to hear him talk about those trips, and I wondered what it would have been like to have today's equipment in those early years.

One particular day while my dad and I explored the south shore of the lake, we came upon a small creek. It was on the NOAA chart, but it was hard to see from the channel because it turned sharply at the entrance. We finally saw it and began idling over to it, only to find the water was too shallow even at high tide.

We both eased out of the boat and pushed and pulled the boat through the shallow water, finding surprisingly deep water at the entrance to the creek. We had no depth finder – my dad would always take a rod and poke it in the water to find the depth. This small creek bottom was deeper than he could reach with his rod, so we started the engine.

The creek wound around to the south to a very small bay and then continued west. The mangroves hung over the water in a canopy fashion, and one or two larger trees lay across the path ahead.

We decided to clear the way, knowing we would be here through the low tide before we could leave. We may as well find a place to fish while we wait! We pushed and pulled mangrove logs and limbs until we could get the boat through the blockage. The creek widened some beyond the blockage.

As we set up under the mangrove trees, we drifted some live shrimp under floats and allowed them to move back toward the undercut bank 30 feet behind the boat. Every time the float reached that bank, it went under as a fish took our shrimp. The take was redfish and snook in the 10-pound range. It was exciting to fight these fish in and out of the mangroves.

On many occasions when the winds howled, and we could not fish any other place, we ended up in this creek. More often than not, we had to get out and push the boat into the creek. And on several occasions, we had to wait an hour or two for the tide to come up far enough to get the boat out. There were also many days that we went directly to this creek, even in good weather, knowing that we could catch fish there.

I mentioned earlier that I might never be able to fish this spot again. The reason is a closure of that entire area to any boat traffic. It seems this area is one of the last breeding areas for the American crocodile, and the National Park Service has taken steps to ensure that the crocs are unencumbered.

I remember those trips as treasures in my life, and I keep those spots secret to this day. It just wouldn't seem right to let someone else fish in my dad's spot.

Secret spots. We all have them. I wonder how many of us have one that we know holds fish, but that we simply can't get to any longer.

The Giant of Little Sable Creek

Such a small creek for such a huge creature…

The west end of Lake Ingraham on the Southwest tip of Florida empties into Middle Cape Canal and then into the Gulf of Mexico. In the lake, just east of the canal is Little Sable Creek, running north into the mangrove and marle prairie. It's a relatively small creek but tends to be deeper than you would think. Tidal currents run in and out of Little Sable, and if it were not so clogged with mangrove logs and limbs, it could be possible to navigate the entire creek up to where it exits to the Gulf several miles to the north.

We never went past the first fork in the creek. A couple of hundred yards into the creek there is a 90-degree fork to the north and east. The north arm was the continuation of the creek at the time. The east arm went another 100 yards or so and tied into the old Raulerson Brothers Canal. With all the other 1920s boondoggle canals, this one was designed to drain the prairie to the north of Lake Ingraham to create farm land. At any rate, we never went any farther than that fork. In the '50s and '60s, neither fork was wide enough to accommodate anything other than a canoe or kayak. But the water at the fork was about 15 feet deep at high tide.

We would idle into the creek on a low tide and stop just before the fork. There was just enough room to get the boat turned around to have the stern facing the fork. We sat there for hours as the tide came in, catching an occasional redfish, a trash-fish in my father's eyes that he quickly released. We caught a variety of trash-fish while we waited for the current to slow.

When the tide slowed and slacked, the two jewfish lines were baited with whatever live, trash-fish we had caught. Both lines went back to the fork, as we waited once again, this time for a jewfish. I never understood why my dad would wait for the tide to stop to put out a bait. It seemed to me that for a jewfish to get to the fork, he had to go right under our boat. Why not put a bait down before the water slacked?

I can't say we always caught a jewfish there, but I know we caught quite a few of them in that creek fork. They were usually under 50-pounds, and that was a good thing for me. They would fit inside the ice chest we had, which meant we could continue fishing. If it was too large for the ice chest, we had to head back in, and fishing would be over for the day. When a fish that large is caught and the weather is hot, as it always is in South Florida, the fish begins to rot and decompose from the inside-out. You can't allow them to sit and bake in the sun. I remember more than one occasion when we gutted a jewfish right there in the boat and cracked some ice up to fill the stomach cavity in an effort to keep the meat. *Note to self: *Never again gut a big fish inside the boat…*

One particular trip found us waiting for the incoming tide to slack. As my dad finished a canned soda, he dropped it into the water beside the boat. Unfortunately, he was never one to worry about the environment. In the '60s he was like most other people in that respect. When people began criticizing him, he simply said he was building an artificial reef. It was late in life before he began any environmental compliance.

The can floated back behind the boat with the current and sort of disappeared into the log jams and mangroves. As we sat and waited for the tide, we heard a crushing, metallic sound. It came from the mangroves behind the boat, and it appeared that something had gotten hold of that soda can.

We looked but could not see anything. A bit later another can was dropped overboard and drifted back. Only, this time we watched the can go all the way back.

To say we were shocked is an understatement. What we saw was a huge American crocodile come out of the log jam and crush the soda can in its jaws. He ate the can!

How cool is that? Is what I thought for about a minute. After that minute, my dad and I began to worry because this gigantic croc was slowly coming up current toward our boat. As my dad pulled in the two jewfish lines, he yelled at me to untie the bow. Then he grabbed the rope starter on the engine and pulled. It took a few pulls to start the engine, and we were able to head out of the creek.

The amazing part of this story is that even with all the yelling and engine noise, the crocodile was not phased in the least. He kept coming right for the boat; I guess he was looking for another food handout. We estimated that he was about 12 feet in length.

I believe that this trip was one of the last we made into this end of Little Sable Creek. We did enter the creek from Gulf a few miles north up the coast, and we did catch some jewfish there. But we never saw any crocodiles on that end.

Sometime later we planned to fish again in the north entrance to the creek. But, when we arrived, we found that pilings had been driven across the mouth of the creek by the National Park Service. The sign posted on the pilings said something about this being a breeding area for the crocodiles, an endangered species, "No Human Presence Allowed." There were pilings with the same warning in the mouth of Turner Creek farther north up the coast as well.

For some reason, they never placed any pilings in the south portion of Little Sable in Lake Ingraham where we encountered our friend. But, that's all right. We were not about to head back in there again anyway.

Little Sable Creek is a shadow of what it used to be on that north shore of Lake Ingraham. It seems that a few hurricanes and tidal surges have helped form another, larger creek that runs the same northerly direction from Middle Cape Canal, and this new creek has taken most of the tidal flow. I have not fished this new creek, and don't even know if it has been named. But, you can see it on Google Earth, and it looks promising! The problem is, the jewfish is now a protected species, and the crocs are still back in there somewhere!

I'll fish the grass flats.

My Soul Mate – My Bride

I firmly believe I was the luckiest man alive when I married my childhood sweetheart…

No one said it would be easy. No one said, "Here are the instructions." But everyone said we would be happy. We investigated life, learned from our mistakes, and grew up together as husband and wife. We were soul mates long before the term was coined.

Susan was my wife, a fisherman's wife. She loved to go with me, as long as we were catching something. I sometimes think she began going with me so that we could be together.

We fished all over South Florida and North Carolina. We caught more fish than should ever be allowed, and in all that time I never heard her complain.

Sometimes the mosquitoes would be so thick in Everglades National Park that we had to cover our mouths to keep from inhaling them. Sometimes the sun was so hot and the wind so still that we sat and baked in the midday sun.

When we were dating in high school, she and I had a standing movie date Saturday night. Her cousin managed a local theatre, and we always had free passes to whatever was playing. We didn't miss many Saturdays.

I would usually fish with my father on any given Saturday. Fishing with him meant we left the house around 4 a.m. and did not get back until about 6 p.m. That's a long, hot day, one that saps your strength like nothing else.

I cut a deal with my dad so I could get home and get to Susan's house to pick her up on time. We left the fish in the ice chest and the boat dirty; I would deal with both issues after church the next day.

I managed to get cleaned up, and we always made it to the movie; seldom were we late. I was in love! But even a star-struck teenager like me could not last long in the dark theatre with comfortable seats. More often than not Susan would end up poking me to wake me up at several points during the movie.

But she never complained. I think she just accepted the fact that I was tired from fishing all day and let it go at that.

My mother warned her just before our wedding that she was going to be second fiddle to a fish. But thankfully, she loved me anyway.

There was the trip where we caught 18 small jewfish in one day from the creeks in Everglades National Park. What made it special was the fact that we caught all of them on Calcutta cane poles. It was legal back then, and there were no limits.

There was the trip that saw us fill not one, but two 120-quart ice chests with mangrove snapper and seatrout. She talked about that one for years.

What made me love her, even more, was her patience and lack of complaining about how bad the mosquitoes were back in those creeks. It was a drizzling, rainy day; we were soaked; and, the mosquitoes came out in force.

She did complain about one of our trips. We made the foolish decision to do some night fishing. We left the dock before sundown and got anchored and set up in an area I thought would produce some big fish. After catching nothing but stingrays, we decided to head back in to the dock. Everything was fine right up to the point that I decided to cut the corner on a flat. We ran aground on a mud and grass flat on an outgoing tide. Not good... We sat there high and dry at 1 o'clock in the morning and watched my cigarette butts still burn on top of the mud. Through her fearful tears, she complained for the first and only time about my fishing.

On one trip back into the mangrove creeks, we decided to take Snoopy, our black and tan, long-hair dachshund. We had him on a leash of sorts in the boat, leaving enough slack for him to walk around. It was hot; the deck of the boat was hot; and, poor Snoopy was miserable.

I guess he was looking for shade when he jumped off the front of the boat. I had run the bow into a mud bank so that we could fish out the back of the boat. You must realize that this mud was soft and thick, and any weight at all would sink into it. That's exactly what happened. Poor Snoop was buried up to his neck in mud. And the more he struggled to get out of it, the deeper he sank. It was all both of us could do to get him back into the boat.

When we fished together, it was a special time. Our last fishing trip before my deployment to Vietnam resulted in her pregnancy with our first son, Tom. I remember being in Chu Lai and getting the letter announcing her pregnancy. "You did it!" she wrote. We had been trying to get pregnant for over two years.

Two years later almost to the day our second son, David, was born, and four years after that our daughter Sara showed up. I went to every store in the small town where we lived and bought any and every pink baby item I could find for Sara. Susan so wished for a daughter.

She sewed for the children, even made me a jacket. Then she sewed for the grandkids. She embroidered everything imaginable. She was a seamstress' seamstress. She loved her family and me more than we knew.

We raised three children together, and I believe it was her strong influence that made each of them what they are today. We had almost 47 years together, and she loved me in spite of every bad thing I ever did.

You may notice that all of this is in the past tense. Cancer is a terrible word. It's a disease that robs us of life if we have it. It robs us of loved ones, soul mates, and friends when someone else has it. It ran in Susan's family on her father's side back several generations.

Early in our marriage, we knew in the back of our minds that the possibility was there. Her sister died of it at 33. But we always rationalized that it might not happen to us. We told people that there was never a question of whether she would get cancer or not; it was a question of when.

"When" happened Dec. 16, 2008. It was three months after her father died of a brain aneurism that we got the call from the hospital's breast cancer clinic. They "saw something" on her recent mammogram and she needed to come back in for a more in-depth look.

We lasted through four and a half years of chemo treatments and radiation as she bravely fought to stay alive. Her biggest fear was that her grandchildren would not remember her, particularly the young ones for whom she sewed.

She kept apologizing to me through her tears, as if she had done something wrong by contracting cancer. She was more concerned about me and my life than she was her own.

We lost her in July 2013, and I miss her more than I ever could have believed I would. "A preacher, a nurse-missionary and a telephone man," she would lay in the bed saying, "We didn't do too badly after all."

She was my soul mate. She was my bride.

Epilogue

Fishing stories are just that – stories. They become a part of you when they are real. They can shape your desires, your beliefs, even your entire life. That's what happened to me over the years. What you have read here paints a pretty good picture of me – my relationship with my dad, my family, a very special friend, and God's wonderful world.

Someone once told me that anyone can fish; only a few people can catch. Well, catch we did and catch we still do, and all within the framework of a loving family while bringing children up to face an ever more complicated world. I feel blessed to have been born with that silver fishhook in my mouth!

ABOUT THE AUTHOR

Ron Brooks is an award winning outdoor writer, having published either in print and online more than 1,000 articles over the past 20 years. He has fished all over the southern U.S. and written about almost all of those experiences. Although he grew up in Key West and South Florida, Ron currently resides in North Florida where he spends his time fishing with his new wife, Donna Jeanne. He is a member and past president of the Georgia Outdoor Writers Association (GOWA) and the Southeastern Outdoor Press Association (SEOPA).

www.ingramcontent.com/pod-product-compliance
Lightning Source LLC
Chambersburg PA
CBHW060014050426
42448CB00012B/2753